The Ultimate Oslo Travel Guide (2025 Edition)

Everything You Need to Know – Top Attractions, Where to Eat, Best Places to Visit & Local Tips

Grace Bennett

Copyright Notice

No part of this book may be reproduced, written, electronic, recorded, or photocopied without written permission from the publisher or author.

The exception would be in the case of brief quotations embodied in critical articles or reviews and pages where permission is specifically granted by the publisher or author.

Although every precaution has been taken to verify the accuracy of the information contained herein, the author and publisher assume no responsibility for any errors or omissions. No liability is assumed for damages that may result from the use of the information contained within.

All Rights Reserved ©2025

The Ultimate Oslo Travel Guide (2025 Edition)

TABLE OF CONTENTS

INTRODUCTION — 7

- Overview of Oslo — 7
- Why Visit Oslo in 2025? — 8
- History and Culture Significance — 9
- Geography and Climate — 10
- How to Use This Guide — 11

CHAPTER 1: TRAVEL ESSENTIALS — 15

- Visa and Entry Requirements — 15
- Currency and Banking — 17
- Language and Communication — 19
- Health and Safety — 21
- Travel Insurance — 23
- Best Time to Visit — 26

CHAPTER 2: PLANNING YOUR TRIP — 29

- The Essential Oslo Packing List — 29
- Packing Tips and Weather Considerations — 31
- Budgeting and Costs — 33
- Budget Travel Tips — 35

CHAPTER 3: GETTING TO OSLO — 39

- By Air — 39
- By Train — 42
- By Bus — 45
- By Car — 48
- By Ferry — 51

CHAPTER 4: GETTING AROUND OSLO — 55

- Public Transportation — 55
- Renting a Car — 58
- Taxis and Ride-Sharing — 60
- Biking in Oslo — 62
- Walking Tours — 65

CHAPTER 5: TOP ATTRACTIONS IN OSLO 69

VIKING SHIP MUSEUM	69
OSLO OPERA HOUSE	72
AKERSHUS FORTRESS	75
VIGELAND PARK (FROGNER PARK)	79
MUNCH MUSEUM	82
THE NORWEGIAN MUSEUM OF CULTURAL HISTORY (NORSK FOLKEMUSEUM)	85
HOLMENKOLLEN SKI JUMP	88
FRAM MUSEUM	91
AKER BRYGGE	94
KON-TIKI MUSEUM	97
ROYAL PALACE	100
OSLO CATHEDRAL (OSLO DOMKIRKE)	103

CHAPTER 6: NEIGHBORHOOD OF OSLO 107

CITY CENTER (SENTRUM)	107
GRÜNERLØKKA	110
AKER BRYGGE AND TJUVHOLMEN	113
MAJORSTUEN	116
FROGNER	119

CHAPTER 7: ACCOMMODATION OPTIONS IN OSLO 123

LUXURY HOTELS	123
TOP 5 LUXURY HOTELS	123
MID-RANGE HOTELS	133
TOP 5 MID-RANGE HOTELS	133
BUDGET ACCOMMODATION	143
TOP 5 BUDGET ACCOMMODATION	143
HOSTELS	153
TOP 5 HOSTELS	153
VACATION RENTALS	163
TOP 5 VACATION RENTALS	163

CHAPTER 8: CULTURAL EXPERIENCES 175

FESTIVALS AND EVENTS	175
THEATRES AND PERFORMING ARTS	178
MUSIC AND CONCERTS	181
ART GALLERIES	184
HISTORICAL SITES	187

OSLO PHILHARMONIC ORCHESTRA 190

CHAPTER 9: OUTDOOR ACTIVITIES AND PARKS 193

HIKING 193
SKIING AND SNOWBOARDING 195
ICE SKATING 198
KAYAKING AND CANOEING 201
CYCLING TRAILS 203
PARKS AND GARDENS 206

CHAPTER 10: SHOPPING IN OSLO 211

SHOPPING STREETS AND DISTRICTS 211
MARKETS AND BAZAARS 215
LOCAL CRAFTS 219
DEPARTMENT STORES AND MALLS 222

Grace Bennett

The Ultimate Oslo Travel Guide (2025 Edition)

INTRODUCTION

Have you ever wondered where you could explore stunning natural landscapes right within a vibrant urban setting? Dreamed of delving into Viking history while enjoying modern Scandinavian culture? Are you looking for a city where you can hike in the morning, visit world-class museums in the afternoon, and dine by the fjord in the evening? Imagine a place where each neighborhood offers a unique charm, from hipster vibes to royal elegance. Are you seeking a destination with efficient public transportation, welcoming locals, and a reputation for safety? Finally, do you want to know the best time to visit, what to pack, and how to make the most of your trip without breaking the bank?

Welcome to Oslo, a city that seamlessly blends nature, history, and modernity, offering an unforgettable experience to every traveler. As the capital of Norway, Oslo is not just a gateway to the country's breathtaking fjords and northern lights; it's a vibrant cultural hub with a rich history, stunning architecture, and a thriving arts scene. Whether you're a history buff, an outdoor enthusiast, a foodie, or simply looking to relax in a beautiful setting, Oslo has something for everyone.

Overview of Oslo

Oslo, the capital city of Norway, is a vibrant and dynamic metropolis that seamlessly blends natural beauty with urban sophistication. Nestled between the Oslofjord and lush, forested hills, Oslo offers a unique combination of outdoor adventures and cultural experiences. As Norway's largest city, it serves as the political, economic, and cultural heart of the country, with a population of over 700,000 residents.

A City of Contrasts

Oslo is renowned for its striking contrasts. Modern architecture and cutting-edge design coexist with historic buildings and ancient Viking sites. The city's skyline is punctuated by the iconic Oslo Opera House, contemporary skyscrapers, and traditional wooden houses, reflecting its rich architectural diversity.

Cultural Hub

Oslo is a cultural powerhouse, boasting an impressive array of museums, galleries, and performance venues. The Munch Museum, home to Edvard Munch's famous painting "The Scream," and the Viking Ship Museum, showcasing well-preserved Viking ships, are must-visit attractions. The city's cultural calendar is packed with events, including the Oslo International Film Festival, Øya Festival, and the Holmenkollen Ski Festival, offering something for every taste.

Green Spaces and Outdoor Activities

Nature is never far away in Oslo. The city is surrounded by pristine forests, parks, and waterways, providing ample opportunities for outdoor activities. Hiking, biking, and skiing are popular pastimes, with the Nordmarka forest and the Holmenkollen ski jump being favorite destinations for locals and tourists alike. In the summer, the Oslofjord's islands are perfect for swimming, kayaking, and picnicking.

Sustainable and Innovative

Oslo is a leader in sustainability and innovation. It was named the European Green Capital in 2019, thanks to its commitment to reducing carbon emissions, promoting green energy, and preserving natural areas. The city's efficient public transportation system, extensive network of bike paths, and focus on electric vehicles make it easy to explore Oslo in an eco-friendly way.

The Ultimate Oslo Travel Guide (2025 Edition)

Gastronomic Delights

Food lovers will find plenty to savor in Oslo. The city's culinary scene is diverse and vibrant, offering everything from traditional Norwegian dishes to international cuisine. Fresh seafood, locally sourced ingredients, and innovative chefs contribute to a dining experience that is both delicious and memorable. Aker Brygge and Tjuvholmen are popular waterfront areas with a plethora of restaurants and cafes to choose from.

Why Oslo?

Visiting Oslo means experiencing a city that offers the best of both worlds: the tranquility of nature and the excitement of a bustling urban center. Whether you're exploring its rich history, indulging in its culinary delights, or simply enjoying the scenic beauty, Oslo promises a memorable and enriching experience.

Why Visit Oslo in 2025?

1. A Year of Cultural Milestones

2025 promises to be a landmark year for Oslo with several key cultural milestones. The city will host numerous special events, exhibitions, and festivals celebrating Norwegian heritage and contemporary arts. The Munch Museum and other cultural institutions are planning unique exhibitions that will only be available this year, providing a once-in-a-lifetime opportunity to experience Oslo's vibrant cultural scene.

2. New Attractions and Developments

Oslo is constantly evolving, with new attractions and developments enhancing its appeal. In 2025, several exciting projects are set to be unveiled, including new museums, public spaces, and architectural marvels. These additions will offer fresh perspectives on Oslo's rich history and innovative future, making it an exciting time to visit.

3. Green Capital Initiatives

As a city known for its commitment to sustainability, Oslo continues to lead in green initiatives. In 2025, the city will introduce new eco-friendly infrastructure and expand its network of green spaces. Visitors can explore Oslo's parks, nature reserves, and urban gardens, enjoying a city that harmoniously blends urban life with nature.

4. Enhanced Connectivity

Traveling to and around Oslo will be easier than ever in 2025. The city is improving its public transportation system with new metro lines, expanded tram services, and increased connectivity to surrounding regions. Enhanced transportation options mean visitors can efficiently explore all that Oslo and its nearby attractions have to offer.

5. Culinary Renaissance

Oslo's culinary scene is undergoing a renaissance, with an influx of new restaurants, food markets, and culinary festivals. In 2025, food enthusiasts can savor an array of gastronomic delights, from traditional Norwegian dishes to international cuisine. The city's focus on locally sourced, sustainable ingredients ensures a dining experience that is both delicious and environmentally conscious.

6. Vibrant Festivals and Events

Oslo's calendar for 2025 is packed with festivals and events that celebrate music, art, film, and more. The Øya Festival, Oslo International Film Festival, and various cultural parades will offer unforgettable experiences for visitors. These events provide a unique opportunity to immerse yourself in the local culture and enjoy world-class entertainment.

7. Ideal Gateway to Norwegian Nature

Oslo is the perfect starting point for exploring Norway's stunning natural landscapes. In 2025, enhanced travel options and guided tours will make it easier than ever to venture into the fjords, mountains, and coastal regions. Whether you're seeking outdoor adventures or tranquil retreats, Oslo offers convenient access to Norway's breathtaking scenery.

8. Commitment to Inclusivity and Innovation

Oslo's dedication to inclusivity and innovation is evident in its diverse cultural offerings and forward-thinking policies. The city embraces modernity while honoring its traditions, creating a welcoming environment for all visitors. In 2025, Oslo's continued focus on innovation will ensure a memorable and enriching travel experience.

With its dynamic blend of history, culture, and natural beauty, Oslo in 2025 is set to offer an unparalleled travel experience. Whether you're a returning visitor or exploring the city for the first time, there's never been a better time to discover all that Oslo has to offer. Plan your trip now and be part of this exciting year in one of Europe's most captivating capitals.

History and Culture Significance

Ancient Origins and Viking Heritage

Oslo's history stretches back over a thousand years, with its founding often attributed to King Harald Hardrada in 1049 AD. However, archaeological evidence suggests that settlements in the area date back even earlier, to the early Middle Ages. This deep history is closely tied to Norway's Viking heritage, and Oslo's roots as a Viking city are celebrated in many of its museums and cultural landmarks. The Viking Ship Museum, housing some of the world's best-preserved Viking ships and artifacts, offers a fascinating glimpse into this era.

Medieval and Renaissance Oslo

In the Middle Ages, Oslo grew in importance as a trading hub and ecclesiastical center. The construction of Akershus Fortress in the late 13th century by King Haakon V significantly enhanced the city's strategic and military importance. The fortress, which has withstood numerous sieges and battles, stands as a testament to Oslo's medieval past and is now a popular historical site.

The Great Fire and Rebirth

Oslo's history is also marked by adversity. In 1624, a devastating fire ravaged the city. King Christian IV of Denmark-Norway ordered the city to be rebuilt closer to Akershus Fortress and renamed it Christiania (later spelled Kristiania). This period saw significant urban development, and many of the city's historic buildings date from this time. The renaming lasted until 1925, when the original name, Oslo, was restored.

Independence and Modern Growth

The dissolution of the union between Norway and Sweden in 1905 marked a new chapter for Oslo as the capital of an independent Norway. The city rapidly developed into a modern European capital, characterized by significant architectural, economic, and cultural growth. Landmarks like the Royal Palace, the National Theatre, and the Parliament building (Stortinget) were constructed during this period, symbolizing Oslo's burgeoning national identity.

Cultural Renaissance

Oslo has a rich cultural tapestry woven from its history, arts, and literature. The city is the birthplace of many renowned figures, including the playwright Henrik Ibsen, whose works are still celebrated worldwide, and the painter Edvard Munch, whose iconic piece "The Scream" is housed in the Munch Museum. Oslo's theaters, galleries, and museums reflect this vibrant cultural heritage.

Contemporary Oslo

Today, Oslo is a bustling metropolis that balances its historical legacy with modern innovation. It has become a hub for sustainable living and green technology, often cited as one of the most environmentally friendly cities in the world. The city's cultural scene is continually evolving, with numerous festivals, concerts, and events that celebrate both its historical roots and contemporary creativity.

Cultural Landmarks and Institutions

Oslo's cultural institutions play a crucial role in preserving and showcasing its heritage. The National Museum, which includes the National Gallery and the Museum of Decorative Arts and Design, is one of the largest art collections in Scandinavia. The Norwegian Museum of Cultural History (Norsk Folkemuseum) on Bygdøy Peninsula offers an open-air experience of traditional Norwegian life.

Oslo's rich history and cultural significance make it a fascinating destination for travelers. From its ancient Viking roots and medieval architecture to its modern innovations and vibrant arts scene, Oslo offers a unique journey through time and culture. Whether you're exploring historical sites, delving into the world of Norwegian art, or experiencing the city's contemporary vibe, Oslo's history and culture are sure to leave a lasting impression.

Geography and Climate

Geography

Oslo, the capital city of Norway, is located in the southeastern part of the country at the head of the Oslofjord, a picturesque inlet that stretches 100 kilometers (62 miles) inland from the Skagerrak strait. The city's unique geographical setting provides a blend of urban and natural environments, making it a compelling destination for travelers seeking both city experiences and outdoor adventures.

The city is surrounded by lush forests and rolling hills, particularly the Marka forests to the north and east, which are popular destinations for hiking, biking, and skiing. To the south, the Oslofjord offers stunning waterfront views and numerous islands that are perfect for day trips and boating excursions. The landscape around Oslo is characterized by its varied terrain, which includes:

Hills and Forests: The city is flanked by the Marka forests, providing a green backdrop and numerous outdoor activity opportunities. These forests are crisscrossed by trails and are accessible year-round for recreational activities.

Waterways: The Oslofjord is a defining feature of the city's geography, with its numerous islands and peninsulas offering both scenic beauty and recreational opportunities.

Urban Greenspaces: Oslo is known for its parks and green spaces, such as Frogner Park and Ekeberg Park, which provide residents and visitors with areas to relax and enjoy nature within the city limits.

Climate

Oslo experiences a temperate climate, characterized by four distinct seasons, each offering unique opportunities for visitors.

Spring (March to May): Spring in Oslo is a time of renewal when the city's parks and gardens come alive with blooming flowers and trees. Temperatures gradually warm up from around 0°C (32°F) in March to 15°C (59°F) in May. It's a great time to explore outdoor attractions as the snow melts and the days grow longer.

Summer (June to August): Summers in Oslo are mild and pleasant, with average temperatures ranging from 15°C (59°F) to 22°C (72°F). The city experiences long daylight hours, with the phenomenon of the midnight sun in June. This is the best time for enjoying outdoor activities such as boating in the Oslofjord, hiking in the nearby forests, or exploring the city's many parks and outdoor cafes.

Autumn (September to November): Autumn brings cooler temperatures, ranging from 10°C (50°F) in September to around 0°C (32°F) by November. The city's parks and forests are ablaze with fall colors, making it a picturesque time to visit. It's also a good time to enjoy cultural attractions like museums and galleries as the weather becomes cooler.

Winter (December to February): Winters in Oslo are cold and snowy, with temperatures often dropping below freezing. Average temperatures range from -5°C (23°F) to 0°C (32°F). Snow is common, creating excellent conditions for winter sports. The city's proximity to ski resorts and its numerous ice skating rinks make it a winter wonderland for outdoor enthusiasts.

Oslo's climate and geography provide a diverse array of experiences for visitors, from summer hikes and fjord cruises to winter skiing and cultural exploration year-round. Whether you are an adventure seeker or a culture lover, Oslo's unique setting and climate ensure that there is always something to enjoy no matter the season.

How to Use This Guide

This guide is designed to be your comprehensive companion as you explore Oslo, ensuring you have all the necessary information to make your trip smooth, enjoyable, and memorable. Here's how to make the most of this guide:

Chapter Structure

Each chapter of this guide focuses on a specific aspect of your trip, from planning and travel essentials to exploring the top attractions and discovering local culture. Here's a quick overview of what you'll find in each chapter:

Introduction to Oslo: Provides a general overview of the city, reasons to visit in 2025, and insights into Oslo's history, culture, geography, and climate.

Chapter 1: Travel Essentials: Covers the basics you need to know before you go, including visa requirements, currency, language, health, and safety tips, and the best time to visit.

Chapter 2: Planning Your Trip: Offers practical advice on packing, budgeting, and travel tips to help you prepare for your journey.

Chapter 3: Getting to Oslo: Details the various ways to reach Oslo, whether by air, train, bus, car, or ferry.

Chapter 4: Getting Around Oslo: Explains the city's public transportation system, car rentals, taxis, biking options, and walking tours.

Chapter 5: Top Attractions in Oslo: Highlights must-see sights and landmarks, from museums and parks to historical sites and modern attractions.

Chapter 6: Neighborhoods of Oslo: Guides you through the diverse areas of Oslo, helping you explore the city's different neighborhoods.

Chapter 7: Accommodation Options in Oslo: Provides information on where to stay, from luxury hotels to budget accommodations and vacation rentals.

Chapter 8: Cultural Experiences: Offers insights into Oslo's festivals, performing arts, music, art galleries, and historical sites.

Chapter 9: Outdoor Activities and Parks: Lists opportunities for hiking, skiing, ice skating, kayaking, cycling, and enjoying Oslo's parks and gardens.

Chapter 10: Shopping in Oslo: Covers the best shopping streets, markets, and places to find local crafts and souvenirs.

Chapter 11: Beaches in Oslo: Details the best beaches and swimming spots in and around the city.

Chapter 12: Food and Drink: Guides you through Oslo's culinary scene, from traditional Norwegian cuisine to street food, cafes, and nightlife.

Chapter 13: Day Trips from Oslo: Suggests exciting day trip destinations around Oslo.

Chapter 14: Essential Itinerary for First-Timers: Provides a 7-day itinerary to help you make the most of your first visit.

Chapter 15: Practical Information: Includes safety tips, emergency contacts, travel etiquette, money-saving tips, and do's and don'ts.

Chapter 16: Conclusion: Offers final tips, useful apps, basic Norwegian phrases, and recommendations for further exploration.

Navigating the Guide

Start with the Introduction: Begin with the "Introduction to Oslo" to get a broad understanding of what the city has to offer and why 2025 is an ideal year to visit.

Use the Table of Contents: Refer to the table of contents to find specific information quickly. Each chapter is self-contained, so you can jump to the section that interests you the most.

Follow the Chapters Sequentially: For a thorough preparation, follow the chapters sequentially. Start with travel essentials, move on to planning and getting to Oslo, then delve into exploring the city's attractions and neighborhoods.

Refer to Practical Information: Use the "Practical Information" chapter for essential travel tips and emergency contacts during your stay.

Customize Your Itinerary: Use the suggested 7-day itinerary as a base, but feel free to customize it based on your interests and the time you have available.

Cultural Insights and Local Tips: Pay attention to the cultural experiences and local tips sections to enrich your visit with authentic experiences.

Stay Updated: Check for any updates or changes in travel requirements, local events, or attraction opening hours that might have occurred since the publication of this guide.

Making the Most of Your Trip

Plan Ahead: Use the planning chapters to organize your trip well in advance, ensuring you have all the necessary documents, reservations, and a well-thought-out itinerary.

Immerse Yourself: Dive into Oslo's culture by visiting museums, attending local festivals, and trying traditional Norwegian dishes.

Explore Outdoors: Take advantage of Oslo's stunning natural surroundings by participating in outdoor activities, whether it's hiking in the Marka forests or kayaking in the Oslofjord.

Stay Flexible: While it's good to have a plan, stay flexible and open to spontaneous discoveries. Some of the best travel experiences happen unexpectedly.

With this guide in hand, you are well-equipped to embark on an unforgettable adventure in Oslo. Enjoy your trip!

The Ultimate Oslo Travel Guide (2025 Edition)

Chapter 1: Travel Essentials

Visa and Entry Requirements

When planning your trip to Oslo, understanding the visa and entry requirements is essential to ensure a smooth and hassle-free journey. Below is a comprehensive guide to help you navigate the process:

Visa Requirements

Schengen Visa

Norway is a member of the Schengen Agreement, which allows travelers to move freely between 26 European countries with a single visa. Depending on your nationality, you may need to apply for a Schengen visa to enter Oslo.

Who Needs a Schengen Visa?

Citizens of non-Schengen countries that do not have a visa-free agreement with the Schengen Area.

Travelers planning to stay in Oslo or any other Schengen country for more than 90 days within a 180-day period.

Who Does Not Need a Schengen Visa?

Citizens of Schengen Area countries.

Citizens of countries with a visa-free agreement with the Schengen Area for short stays (up to 90 days within a 180-day period).

Application Process

Determine Your Visa Type: Most tourists will need a short-stay Schengen visa (Type C). If you plan to study, work, or stay longer, other types of visas may apply.

Gather Required Documents: Typical documents include a completed application form, a valid passport, passport-sized photos, travel itinerary, proof of accommodation, travel insurance, proof of financial means, and a cover letter explaining your purpose of visit.

Schedule an Appointment: Submit your application at the nearest Norwegian embassy or consulate. Some countries have visa application centers that handle this process.

Pay the Visa Fee: The fee for a short-stay Schengen visa is approximately €80, though it may vary based on your nationality or specific circumstances.

Attend the Visa Interview: Be prepared to discuss your travel plans and provide additional documentation if requested.

Processing Time

Visa processing times can vary, but it typically takes around 15 calendar days. It's advisable to apply well in advance of your planned travel date to account for any delays.

The Ultimate Oslo Travel Guide (2025 Edition)

Entry Requirements

Passport Validity

- Ensure your passport is:
- Valid for at least three months beyond your intended departure date from the Schengen Area.
- Issued within the last ten years.

Border Control

Upon arrival in Oslo, you will go through border control where you will need to present:

- A valid passport or travel document.
- A valid visa (if applicable).
- Proof of sufficient funds for your stay.
- Return or onward travel tickets.
- Proof of accommodation.

Customs Regulations

Restricted and Prohibited Items: Norway has strict regulations on certain items, including firearms, drugs, and endangered species. Familiarize yourself with these regulations to avoid any issues at customs.

Duty-Free Allowance: Travelers are allowed to bring certain quantities of alcohol, tobacco, and other goods duty-free. Check the latest allowances before you travel.

Health and COVID-19 Regulations

Vaccinations: No specific vaccinations are required for entry into Norway, but it's always good to check the latest health advisories.

COVID-19: Depending on the global situation, there may be specific entry requirements related to COVID-19, such as vaccination proof, testing, or quarantine. Ensure you are aware of the latest guidelines before you travel.

Tips for a Smooth Entry

Prepare Documentation: Keep all necessary documents organized and readily accessible.

Be Honest and Clear: Answer all questions at border control truthfully and clearly.

Stay Informed: Regulations can change, so check for updates from official sources such as the Norwegian Directorate of Immigration (UDI) and your local embassy.

Currency and Banking

When traveling to Oslo, understanding the local currency and banking system will help you manage your finances efficiently. Here's what you need to know:

Currency

Norwegian Krone (NOK)

The official currency of Norway is the Norwegian Krone, abbreviated as NOK. Here's a quick overview:

Symbol: kr

Banknotes: 50, 100, 200, 500, and 1000 kr

Coins: 1, 5, 10, and 20 kr

Exchange Rates

Exchange rates fluctuate, so it's a good idea to check the current rate before you travel. You can exchange your currency for NOK at banks, currency exchange offices, and at Oslo's airport.

Banking

ATMs

ATMs, known locally as minibanks, are widely available throughout Oslo, including at the airport, major train stations, and around the city center. Most ATMs accept international debit and credit cards such as Visa, MasterCard, and Maestro. Using an ATM is often one of the most convenient and cost-effective ways to obtain Norwegian currency.

Tips for Using ATMs:

Notify your bank of your travel plans to avoid any security holds on your account.

Check with your bank about international withdrawal fees.

Opt for ATMs located in well-lit, secure areas.

Credit and Debit Cards

Credit and debit cards are widely accepted in Oslo, including in hotels, restaurants, shops, and taxis. Visa and MasterCard are the most commonly accepted, with American Express and Diners Club also accepted in many places.

Tips for Using Cards:

Use cards with chip-and-PIN technology for added security.

Keep a small amount of cash on hand for smaller establishments or markets that may not accept cards.

Monitor your account for any unauthorized transactions.

Banks and Banking Hours

Banks in Oslo typically operate Monday to Friday from 9:00 AM to 3:00 PM. Some branches may have extended hours on certain days or offer services by appointment. Major banks in Oslo include DNB, Nordea, and SpareBank 1.

Services Provided:

Currency exchange

International money transfers

General banking services

Mobile Payments

Norway is a leader in adopting digital payments, and mobile payment solutions like Vipps are popular. Vipps allows users to transfer money, pay for goods and services, and even pay bills directly from their smartphones. It's widely accepted in Oslo, so consider setting it up if you plan to stay in Norway for an extended period.

Currency Exchange

Where to Exchange Currency

Banks: Offer competitive exchange rates but may charge a service fee.

Currency Exchange Offices: Available at Oslo Gardermoen Airport and in the city center.

ATMs: Often provide the best rates with minimal fees.

Tips for Currency Exchange:

Compare rates and fees at different locations.

Avoid exchanging money at hotels, where rates are typically less favorable.

Keep receipts for record-keeping and potential reversals.

Traveler's Checks

Traveler's checks are not commonly used in Norway. While some banks may cash them, it's more convenient to rely on ATMs, credit/debit cards, and mobile payments.

Tax Refunds

As a visitor to Norway, you may be eligible for a VAT refund on purchases made in the country. Look for stores displaying the "Tax-Free Shopping" logo and ask for a tax-free form when you make a purchase. You can claim your refund at the airport before departure.

Steps for Claiming Tax Refunds:

Present your passport when shopping.

Complete the tax-free form provided by the retailer.

Show the completed form, along with your purchases and receipts, at the refund counter at the airport.

Financial Tips for Travelers

Keep Multiple Payment Options: Carry a mix of cash, cards, and mobile payment options.

Monitor Exchange Rates: Exchange currency when rates are favorable.

Stay Informed About Fees: Be aware of any international transaction fees your bank may charge.

Secure Your Finances: Use secure ATMs, keep an eye on your cards, and report any suspicious activity immediately.

Language and Communication

Navigating language and communication in Oslo is essential for a smooth and enjoyable travel experience. Here's a comprehensive guide to help you understand and communicate effectively in the Norwegian capital.

Official Language

Norwegian

Norwegian (Norsk) is the official language of Norway. It has two written forms:

Bokmål: The most commonly used form, especially in Oslo.

Nynorsk: Used more frequently in rural areas and western Norway.

Despite the differences, both forms are mutually intelligible, and you'll primarily encounter Bokmål in Oslo.

English Proficiency

Norwegians are known for their excellent English skills. Most people in Oslo, especially in the hospitality and service industries, speak English fluently. You'll find that menus, signs, and information in tourist areas are often available in both Norwegian and English.

Useful Tips:

Don't hesitate to speak English; locals are generally friendly and willing to help.

Learn a few basic Norwegian phrases; it shows respect and can enhance your experience.

Basic Norwegian Phrases

Learning a few basic phrases can go a long way in making your trip more enjoyable. Here are some useful expressions:

Hello: Hei

Goodbye: Ha det

Please: Vær så snill

Thank you: Takk

Yes: Ja

No: Nei

Excuse me/Sorry: Unnskyld

Do you speak English?: Snakker du engelsk?

How much does it cost?: Hvor mye koster det?

Where is…?: Hvor er…?

Communication Tips

Mobile Phones

Norway has a well-developed mobile network, and you can use your phone easily in Oslo. Here are some options:

Roaming: Check with your provider about international roaming packages.

Local SIM Card: Consider purchasing a local SIM card for better rates on calls, texts, and data.

eSIM: Some newer phones support eSIMs, which can be a convenient option.

Internet Access

Wi-Fi: Widely available in hotels, cafes, restaurants, and public spaces. Look for "Oslo Wi-Fi" hotspots around the city.

Mobile Data: If you have a local SIM or a good roaming package, you can rely on mobile data for internet access.

Postal Services

If you need to send postcards or packages, Oslo's postal services are efficient and reliable. Post offices (Posten) are located throughout the city, and you can also buy stamps at many convenience stores.

Emergency Contacts

Emergency Number: 112 (Police), 113 (Ambulance), 110 (Fire)

Tourist Information: Oslo Visitor Centre can provide assistance and information.

Useful Apps for Travelers

Google Translate: Great for instant translations.

Oslo City App: Provides information on attractions, events, and navigation.

RuterReise: For public transportation schedules and routes.

Vipps: Mobile payment app widely used in Norway.

Cultural Communication Tips

Politeness: Norwegians value politeness and directness. Being straightforward yet courteous will be appreciated.

Personal Space: Respect personal space and avoid standing too close to people in queues or public places.

Greetings: A firm handshake with eye contact is a common greeting.

Health and Safety

Ensuring your health and safety while traveling is crucial for a worry-free and enjoyable experience. Here's a comprehensive guide to help you stay healthy and safe during your visit to Oslo.

Health

Medical Facilities

Oslo boasts high-quality healthcare facilities, including hospitals, clinics, and pharmacies. In case of a medical emergency, you can expect prompt and professional care.

Hospitals:

Oslo University Hospital (Oslo Universitetssykehus): The largest and most comprehensive hospital in the city, offering a wide range of medical services.

Diakonhjemmet Hospital (Diakonhjemmet Sykehus): Known for its excellent care and specialized services.

Pharmacies

Pharmacies, known as "Apotek" in Norwegian, are widely available throughout Oslo. Most pharmacists speak English and can assist with over-the-counter medications and prescriptions.

Pharmacy Chains:

Apotek 1

Vitusapotek

Boots Apotek

Health Insurance

It's highly recommended to have comprehensive travel health insurance before you travel to Oslo. Ensure your insurance covers:

Medical treatment and hospitalization

Emergency evacuation and repatriation

Coverage for pre-existing conditions, if applicable

Vaccinations

No specific vaccinations are required for entry into Norway. However, it's advisable to be up-to-date on routine vaccinations, such as:

- Measles, Mumps, Rubella (MMR)
- Diphtheria, Tetanus, Pertussis (DTP)
- Influenza

COVID-19 Considerations

Depending on the global situation, COVID-19 regulations may vary. Check the latest travel advisories and guidelines from Norwegian health authorities before your trip.

Water and Food Safety

Tap Water: Safe to drink and of high quality.

Food Safety: Oslo has stringent food safety regulations. Street food and restaurant meals are generally safe to consume.

Safety

General Safety

Oslo is considered one of the safest cities in Europe. Violent crime is rare, and the city has a low crime rate. However, it's always wise to take standard precautions.

Safety Tips

Personal Belongings: Keep your valuables secure and be aware of your surroundings, especially in crowded areas.

Pickpocketing: Be cautious in tourist hotspots and public transportation where pickpocketing can occur.

Emergency Contacts: Save local emergency numbers on your phone.

Emergency Numbers

Police: 112

Ambulance: 113

Fire: 110

Natural Disasters

Norway experiences few natural disasters. However, it's good to be aware of the following:

Winter Conditions: In winter, be cautious of icy sidewalks and roads. Wear appropriate footwear and drive carefully.

Hiking Safety: If hiking in the surrounding areas, inform someone of your plans and check weather forecasts.

Travel Insurance

Having comprehensive travel insurance is essential. Ensure it covers:

- Medical emergencies
- Trip cancellations
- Lost or stolen belongings

- Adventure activities, if you plan to partake

Public Health Services

Public health services in Oslo are excellent. In addition to hospitals and clinics, you can find numerous health centers providing various medical services.

Mental Health Services

If you require mental health support during your stay, several resources are available:

Oslo Crisis Center (Oslo Krisesenter): Provides support for individuals in crisis.

Mental Health Services: Available through hospitals and specialized clinics.

Health and Safety Apps

Helsenorge: Provides information about healthcare services in Norway.

112 App: Can be used to quickly contact emergency services.

RuterReise: For public transportation information.

Travel Insurance

Travel insurance is an essential component of your trip planning to Oslo, providing financial protection and peace of mind in case of unexpected events. Here's a detailed guide to help you understand the importance of travel insurance and what to look for when purchasing a policy.

Why You Need Travel Insurance

Medical Emergencies

Even though Oslo has excellent healthcare facilities, medical treatments can be expensive, especially for non-residents. Travel insurance covers:

Emergency medical treatment

Hospitalization

Medical evacuation and repatriation

Trip Cancellations and Interruptions

Life is unpredictable, and unforeseen circumstances can lead to trip cancellations or interruptions. Travel insurance typically covers:

Trip cancellations due to illness, injury, or death of a family member

Trip interruptions caused by severe weather, natural disasters, or strikes

Non-refundable expenses such as flights, accommodations, and tours

Lost or Stolen Belongings

Luggage can be lost, and valuables can be stolen. Travel insurance provides coverage for:

Lost, stolen, or damaged luggage

Theft of personal belongings such as passports, cameras, and electronics

Delayed baggage

Travel Delays

Travel delays can disrupt your itinerary and incur additional expenses. Insurance can cover:

Additional accommodation and meal costs

Costs incurred due to missed connections

Liability Coverage

In case you accidentally cause injury to someone or damage their property, travel insurance may include personal liability coverage.

Types of Travel Insurance

Single-Trip Insurance

This policy covers one specific trip. It's ideal for:

Short vacations

Business trips

Multi-Trip (Annual) Insurance

This policy covers multiple trips within a year. It's suitable for:

Frequent travelers

Business travelers with multiple international trips

Specialized Travel Insurance

For those engaging in specific activities, such as adventure sports or skiing, specialized policies are available to cover risks associated with these activities.

What to Look for in a Travel Insurance Policy

Coverage Limits

Ensure the policy offers sufficient coverage for medical expenses, trip cancellations, and lost belongings. Check the maximum limits for each type of coverage.

Exclusions

Understand what is not covered by the policy. Common exclusions include:

Pre-existing medical conditions

Injuries from high-risk activities (unless specifically covered)

Losses due to negligence

Deductibles

Check the deductible amounts for each type of coverage. A higher deductible might lower your premium but will require you to pay more out of pocket in case of a claim.

Claim Process

A straightforward and efficient claim process is crucial. Look for:

24/7 customer support

Online claim submission options

Clear guidelines on required documentation

Policy Extensions

Consider if the policy allows extensions for:

Prolonged stays

Coverage for additional activities

How to Purchase Travel Insurance

Compare Policies

Use comparison websites to evaluate different policies based on coverage, price, and customer reviews.

Buy Early

Purchase travel insurance as soon as you book your trip to ensure coverage for any unforeseen events that might occur before your departure.

Tailor Your Policy

Customize your policy to suit your specific needs, such as adding coverage for adventure sports or higher coverage limits for expensive electronics.

Read the Fine Print

Carefully read the policy documents to fully understand the coverage, exclusions, and claim process.

Recommended Travel Insurance Providers

Some well-known travel insurance providers include:

World Nomads: Known for flexible and comprehensive coverage, especially for adventure travelers.

Allianz Global Assistance: Offers a wide range of plans and excellent customer service.

AXA Assistance: Provides extensive coverage options and a straightforward claims process.

InsureMyTrip: A comparison site that helps you find the best policy based on your needs.

Best Time to Visit

Oslo, with its rich cultural offerings and beautiful natural surroundings, is a year-round destination. The best time to visit depends on your interests and the experiences you seek. Here's a guide to help you choose the ideal time for your trip to Oslo.

Seasonal Overview

Spring (March to May)

Weather: Spring in Oslo brings gradually warming temperatures and the melting of winter snow. Average temperatures range from 0°C (32°F) in March to 12°C (54°F) in May.

Highlights:

Cherry Blossoms: Enjoy the cherry blossoms in the city's parks, particularly in Frogner Park.

Outdoor Activities: Perfect weather for hiking and exploring the city's parks and green spaces.

Cultural Events: Spring is a great time to experience cultural events and festivals, including the Oslo Jazz Festival.

Advantages:

Fewer tourists compared to summer.

Mild weather with the onset of longer daylight hours.

Summer (June to August)

Weather: Summer in Oslo is warm and pleasant, with temperatures ranging from 15°C (59°F) to 22°C (72°F). The days are long, with up to 19 hours of daylight in June.

Highlights:

Outdoor Festivals: Oslo hosts a variety of festivals, including the Øya Festival and Oslo Pride.

Sightseeing: Enjoy the city's many outdoor attractions, such as the Oslo Opera House and the Bygdøy Peninsula.

Archipelago Visits: Take boat trips to explore the Oslofjord's islands.

Advantages:

Ideal weather for outdoor activities and sightseeing.

Long daylight hours provide more time for exploration.

Considerations:

Peak tourist season, so expect larger crowds and higher prices for accommodations.

Autumn (September to November)

Weather: Autumn sees temperatures dropping from around 14°C (57°F) in September to 2°C (36°F) in November. The city experiences colorful fall foliage and shorter days.

The Ultimate Oslo Travel Guide (2025 Edition)

Highlights:

Autumn Colors: Enjoy the vibrant fall colors in Oslo's parks and forests.

Cultural Season: The Oslo International Chamber Music Festival and various theater productions take place.

Fewer Crowds: Less crowded than summer, providing a more relaxed experience.

Advantages:

Beautiful fall scenery and milder weather compared to winter.

Lower accommodation prices and fewer tourists.

Winter (December to February)

Weather: Winter in Oslo is cold, with temperatures ranging from -10°C (14°F) to 2°C (36°F). Snow is common, and daylight is limited to about 6 hours per day.

Highlights:

Winter Sports: Excellent conditions for skiing and snowboarding at nearby resorts like Holmenkollen.

Holiday Festivities: Enjoy Christmas markets, festive lights, and New Year celebrations.

Northern Lights: While not guaranteed, there's a chance to see the Northern Lights in northern parts of Norway.

Advantages:

Winter sports and activities are at their peak.

Festive atmosphere with Christmas markets and events.

Considerations:

Cold temperatures and shorter days may limit sightseeing.

Be prepared for winter weather conditions and possible travel disruptions.

Special Events and Festivals

Oslo International Film Festival (November): A major film event featuring international cinema.

Oslo Design Fair (January/February and August): A prominent event for design enthusiasts.

Frognerparken's Summer Concerts (Summer): Enjoy outdoor music performances in a picturesque setting.

Grace Bennett

Chapter 2: Planning Your Trip
The Essential Oslo Packing List

When preparing for a vacation to Oslo, packing appropriately will ensure that you are comfortable and well-prepared for the city's diverse weather conditions and activities. Here's a comprehensive packing list to help you get ready for your trip:

Clothing

Seasonal Clothing

Winter:

Warm, insulated coat or down jacket

Thermal layers (base layers, thermal underwear)

Woolen sweaters or fleeces

Waterproof and windproof outer layer

Warm hat, gloves, and scarf

Thermal socks and waterproof boots

Spring/Fall:

Light to medium-weight coat or jacket

Layerable clothing (sweaters, long-sleeve shirts)

Comfortable jeans or pants

Light waterproof jacket or umbrella

Warm hat and gloves (for cooler days)

Summer:

Lightweight, breathable clothing

Light jacket or sweater for cooler evenings

Comfortable walking shoes or sandals

Sun hat or cap

Sunglasses

Swimwear (if visiting beaches or pools)

General Clothing Items

Casual wear (t-shirts, jeans, and shorts)

Dressy outfit for formal occasions or dining

Pajamas and undergarments

Comfortable walking shoes

Footwear

Walking Shoes: Comfortable shoes for exploring the city.

Waterproof Shoes: Especially useful in rainy weather or for winter conditions.

Casual Shoes: For dining or casual outings.

Accessories

Umbrella: Compact and durable for unexpected rain showers.

Travel Backpack or Daypack: For daily excursions and carrying essentials.

Reusable Water Bottle: To stay hydrated while exploring.

Toiletries

Personal Care Items: Toothbrush, toothpaste, deodorant, shampoo, conditioner, soap or body wash.

Moisturizer and Lip Balm: To combat dry weather, especially in winter.

Sunscreen: For protection against UV rays, even in cooler weather.

Medication: Any prescription or over-the-counter medication you might need.

Electronics

Smartphone and Charger: Essential for communication and navigation.

Camera: For capturing memories of your trip.

Travel Adapter: Norway uses Type C and Type F plugs with a standard voltage of 230V. Ensure your devices are compatible or bring an appropriate adapter.

Laptop or Tablet: If needed for work or leisure.

Documents

Passport: Valid for at least three months beyond your departure date.

Travel Insurance: Policy documents and emergency contact numbers.

Visa: If required, ensure you have your visa and any related documentation.

Travel Itinerary: Details of your accommodation, flight information, and any bookings or reservations.

Copies of Important Documents: Keep photocopies or digital backups of your passport, visa, and travel insurance in case of loss.

The Ultimate Oslo Travel Guide (2025 Edition)

Health and Safety

First Aid Kit: Basic supplies for minor injuries or ailments.

Hand Sanitizer: Useful for maintaining hygiene, especially when traveling.

Money and Cards

Credit/Debit Cards: For easy transactions and emergency funds.

Cash: Norwegian Krone (NOK) for small purchases and places that may not accept cards.

Optional Items

Travel Guide or Map: For navigating the city and discovering local attractions.

Travel Pillow: For comfort during flights or long train journeys.

Binoculars: If you're interested in bird watching or sightseeing from a distance.

Notebook and Pen: For jotting down travel notes or journal entries.

Packing Tips and Weather Considerations

Packing Tips

1. Layer Your Clothing

Oslo's weather can vary significantly, even within a single day. Layering your clothing allows you to adjust to changing temperatures easily.

Suggested Layers:

Base Layer: Moisture-wicking, thermal, or breathable fabrics to keep you comfortable.

Middle Layer: Insulating layers like fleece or sweaters for warmth.

Outer Layer: Waterproof and windproof jacket to protect against rain and wind.

2. Pack Versatile Clothing

Choose versatile clothing items that can be mixed and matched for different occasions and weather conditions.

Examples:

Neutral Colors: Easier to mix and match.

Multi-purpose Items: A dress that can be dressed up or down, or pants that can double as casual or formal wear.

3. Choose Comfortable Footwear

Comfortable and durable shoes are essential for exploring Oslo's various attractions and walking tours.

Types:

Walking Shoes: For daily sightseeing and city exploration.

Waterproof Shoes: Especially useful in rainy or snowy conditions.

Casual Shoes: For dining and social outings.

4. Use Packing Cubes or Compression Bags

Packing cubes or compression bags help keep your luggage organized and save space. They also make it easier to find what you need without unpacking everything.

5. Keep Essentials Accessible

Pack essential items in an easily accessible part of your luggage, such as:

Travel Documents: Passport, visa, and travel insurance.

Medication: Any necessary prescriptions or over-the-counter medicine.

Valuables: Keep your wallet, phone, and camera in a secure but accessible place.

6. Prepare for Rain and Snow

Oslo can experience rain or snow depending on the season, so be prepared:

Rain Gear: Include a compact umbrella and a waterproof jacket.

Snow Gear: For winter visits, pack thermal socks, insulated gloves, and a warm hat.

Weather Considerations

Spring (March to May)

Temperature: Ranges from 0°C (32°F) to 12°C (54°F).

Weather: Transition from cold to mild, with occasional rain and possible late snow.

Packing Tips: Light to medium-weight coat, layering options, and an umbrella for spring showers.

Summer (June to August)

Temperature: Ranges from 15°C (59°F) to 22°C (72°F).

Weather: Warm and pleasant with long daylight hours.

Packing Tips: Lightweight clothing, sun protection (hat, sunglasses, sunscreen), and a light jacket for cooler evenings.

Autumn (September to November)

Temperature: Ranges from 14°C (57°F) in September to 2°C (36°F) in November.

Weather: Cooling temperatures with increasing chance of rain and early snow.

Packing Tips: Medium to warm layers, a waterproof jacket, and warm accessories like hats and gloves.

Winter (December to February)

Temperature: Ranges from -10°C (14°F) to 2°C (36°F).

Weather: Cold with snow and limited daylight.

Packing Tips: Insulated coat, thermal layers, waterproof boots, warm hat, gloves, and a scarf.

Additional Weather Tips

Check Forecasts: Always check the weather forecast before your trip to make any necessary adjustments to your packing list.

Stay Informed: Pay attention to local weather updates, especially if you plan to engage in outdoor activities or travel outside the city.

Budgeting and Costs

Understanding the costs associated with visiting Oslo helps you plan your trip more effectively and manage your budget. Oslo is known for being one of the more expensive cities in Europe, but with proper planning, you can make the most of your visit without overspending. Here's a comprehensive guide to budgeting for your trip to Oslo.

Accommodation Costs

Types of Accommodation

Luxury Hotels: Prices for high-end hotels like the Grand Hotel or The Thief typically range from NOK 2,000 to NOK 5,000 per night.

Mid-Range Hotels: Expect to pay between NOK 1,200 and NOK 2,000 per night for a comfortable stay at places like the Radisson Blu or Thon Hotel.

Budget Accommodation: Hostels and budget hotels generally cost between NOK 500 and NOK 1,200 per night.

Vacation Rentals: Airbnb and similar services offer a range of options from NOK 800 to NOK 2,000 per night depending on the size and location.

Dining Costs

Types of Dining

High-End Restaurants: Fine dining establishments can cost between NOK 500 and NOK 1,500 per person for a meal.

Mid-Range Restaurants: A meal at a mid-range restaurant typically costs between NOK 200 and NOK 400 per person.

Budget Options: Fast food and casual eateries generally range from NOK 100 to NOK 200 per meal.

Self-Catering: If you choose to buy groceries and cook your own meals, expect to spend about NOK 500 to NOK 800 per week for basic groceries.

Transportation Costs

Public Transportation

Single Ticket: A single ride on the bus, tram, or metro costs about NOK 42.

24-Hour Pass: Unlimited travel for 24 hours costs around NOK 130.

7-Day Pass: Unlimited travel for 7 days costs approximately NOK 330.

Taxis and Ride-Sharing

Taxi Fare: The initial fare is around NOK 100, with an additional NOK 15-20 per kilometer.

Ride-Sharing: Services like Uber are available and might offer slightly cheaper rates compared to taxis.

Car Rental

Daily Rental: Prices typically range from NOK 500 to NOK 1,000 per day depending on the car type and rental company.

Attractions and Activities

Entrance Fees

Viking Ship Museum: Approximately NOK 120.

Oslo Opera House: Free to explore the exterior; guided tours cost around NOK 150.

Akershus Fortress: Around NOK 100.

Vigeland Park: Free entry.

Munch Museum: Approximately NOK 140.

Tours and Excursions

City Tours: Guided city tours generally cost between NOK 300 and NOK 600.

Fjord Cruises: Prices for a fjord cruise range from NOK 400 to NOK 800.

Shopping

Souvenirs: Expect to pay around NOK 100 to NOK 500 for typical souvenirs like postcards, keychains, and local crafts.

Clothing and Accessories: Prices vary widely depending on the store and brand. Budget around NOK 500 to NOK 1,500 for shopping.

Miscellaneous Costs

Tips and Gratuities

Restaurants: Tipping is not obligatory but appreciated; a 5-10% tip is customary if service is not included.

Hotels: It is not common to tip hotel staff, but rounding up the bill or leaving small change is appreciated.

Emergency Expenses

Medical: Ensure you have travel insurance to cover any unforeseen medical expenses.

Miscellaneous: Budget an extra NOK 500 to NOK 1,000 for unexpected expenses or emergencies.

Money-Saving Tips

City Pass: Consider purchasing an Oslo Pass if you plan to visit multiple attractions. It provides free entry to many museums and free public transportation.

Grocery Stores: Buy snacks and drinks from grocery stores rather than convenience stores to save money.

Lunch Specials: Many restaurants offer lunch specials or cheaper meal deals, which can be a great way to enjoy dining out at a lower cost.

Budget Travel Tips

Traveling to Oslo doesn't have to break the bank. With some planning and smart choices, you can enjoy the city's attractions, culture, and experiences without overspending. Here are some budget travel tips to help you save money while making the most of your trip.

1. Opt for Budget Accommodation

Hostels: Consider staying in hostels for affordable rates. Many offer private rooms as well.

Vacation Rentals: Use platforms like Airbnb or Booking.com to find budget-friendly rentals. Staying in a rental can also save you money on dining by allowing you to cook your own meals.

Budget Hotels: Look for budget hotels or motels that offer competitive rates. Check reviews to ensure you're getting good value for your money.

2. Use Public Transportation

Oslocard: Purchase an Oslo Travel Pass or an Oslocard for unlimited travel on public transportation. It's more cost-effective than buying single tickets.

City Bikes: Oslo offers bike-sharing services, which can be a cheap and enjoyable way to explore the city.

Walk: Many of Oslo's attractions are within walking distance of each other. Exploring on foot can save on transportation costs and provide a more immersive experience.

3. Take Advantage of Free Attractions

Parks and Gardens: Enjoy free access to Oslo's beautiful parks, such as Vigeland Park and the Oslo Botanical Garden.

City Walks: Explore historic areas like the Aker Brygge and the waterfront on foot.

Museums: Some museums offer free entry on certain days or times. Check their websites for details.

4. Eat Like a Local

Street Food: Try local street food for affordable and tasty meals. Hot dogs and other street food options are budget-friendly.

Lunch Specials: Many restaurants offer lunch specials or set menus at lower prices compared to dinner.

Supermarkets: Buy groceries from supermarkets and prepare your own meals. This can be a significant cost saver compared to eating out for every meal.

5. Shop Smart

Discount Stores: Visit discount stores or outlets for affordable clothing and souvenirs.

Souvenirs: Look for local markets or shops where you can find budget-friendly souvenirs and gifts.

6. Plan and Book in Advance

Early Booking: Book accommodations and major attractions in advance to secure lower prices and availability.

Discounts: Look for online discounts and deals on activities and tours. Websites like Groupon or local deal sites may offer special promotions.

7. Use City Passes

Oslo Pass: Consider purchasing the Oslo Pass if you plan to visit multiple attractions. It offers free or discounted entry to many museums and attractions, as well as free public transportation.

8. Travel Off-Peak

Timing: Visit during the shoulder seasons (spring and fall) when prices for accommodations and flights may be lower, and attractions are less crowded.

Flights: Book flights during off-peak times or use fare comparison tools to find the best deals.

9. Stay Informed

Local Events: Check local event listings for free or low-cost events and activities happening during your visit.

Tourist Information Centers: Visit tourist information centers for free maps, brochures, and advice on budget-friendly activities.

10. Save on Entrance Fees

Combined Tickets: Some attractions offer combined tickets or multi-attraction passes that can save you money.

Student or Senior Discounts: If you qualify, look for student or senior discounts on tickets and admission fees.

11. Avoid Unnecessary Fees

Foreign Transaction Fees: Use a credit or debit card that doesn't charge foreign transaction fees.

ATM Fees: Use ATMs that are part of your bank's network to avoid high withdrawal fees.

12. Practice Smart Spending

Budget Tracking: Keep track of your spending to stay within your budget.

Set Daily Limits: Set daily spending limits to ensure you don't overspend during your trip.

Chapter 3: Getting to Oslo
By Air

Traveling to Oslo by air is a convenient and efficient way to reach Norway's capital from virtually anywhere in the world. Here's a comprehensive guide on how to navigate this route, including major airports, airlines, arrival procedures, and travel tips.

Major Airports

Oslo Gardermoen Airport (OSL)

Location: Approximately 35 kilometers (22 miles) north of Oslo's city center.

Facilities: The largest and busiest airport in Norway, offering a wide range of services including shopping, dining, lounges, and car rental.

Transportation to City Center:

Train: The Airport Express Train (Flytoget) provides a quick and direct connection to Oslo Central Station in about 20 minutes.

Bus: Several bus services operate between the airport and various locations in Oslo.

Taxi: Taxis are available outside the arrivals terminal, with a journey to the city center taking around 40 minutes.

Car Rental: Various car rental agencies are located at the airport.

Oslo Rygge Airport (RYG)

Location: Approximately 60 kilometers (37 miles) southeast of Oslo.

Facilities: Smaller than Gardermoen but offers essential services like shops and dining.

Transportation to City Center:

Train: Rygge Station connects with Oslo Central Station in about an hour. Shuttle buses may also be available.

Bus: Several bus companies operate services between the airport and Oslo.

Taxi: Available, but more expensive and time-consuming compared to other options.

Oslo Torp Airport (TRF)

Location: About 110 kilometers (68 miles) south of Oslo.

Facilities: Basic facilities including shops and dining options.

Transportation to City Center:

Train: Shuttle buses connect the airport with Sandefjord Station, where you can catch a train to Oslo Central Station.

Bus: Direct buses to Oslo take approximately 1.5 to 2 hours.

Taxi: More expensive and less convenient compared to other transportation options.

Airlines and Flights

Major Airlines Flying to Oslo

Norwegian Air Shuttle: Offers a range of domestic and international flights, often providing competitive prices and frequent service.

SAS (Scandinavian Airlines): Provides numerous flights to Oslo from major cities across Europe and beyond.

KLM: Offers flights from various international destinations with connections through Amsterdam.

British Airways: Connects Oslo with London and other UK cities.

Lufthansa: Provides flights from Germany and other European destinations.

Booking Tips

Book in Advance: To secure the best fares and availability, book your flight several months in advance.

Compare Airlines: Use comparison websites to find the best deals and flight options.

Check Baggage Policies: Different airlines have varying baggage policies, so ensure you understand the rules regarding carry-on and checked luggage.

Arrival Procedures

Customs and Immigration

Passport Control: Present your passport and any required visas at the immigration desk. Citizens of EU/EEA countries, the US, and many other nations do not require a visa for short stays.

Customs Declaration: Declare any items that exceed the duty-free limits or are prohibited. Norway follows EU customs regulations.

Baggage Claim

Baggage Carousel: Follow signs to the baggage claim area to collect your checked luggage.

Lost Luggage: If your luggage is missing or damaged, report it to the airline's lost baggage counter.

Health and Safety

Travel Insurance: Ensure you have travel insurance that covers medical emergencies and other potential issues.

COVID-19 Regulations: Follow any specific health and safety guidelines in place, including vaccination or testing requirements.

Transportation from the Airport

Oslo Gardermoen Airport (OSL)

Train: The Flytoget Airport Express Train and Vy regional trains offer fast connections to the city center.

The Ultimate Oslo Travel Guide (2025 Edition)

Bus: The Flybussen and local bus services connect various parts of Oslo.

Taxi: Available at designated taxi stands.

Car Rental: Rental agencies are located in the airport terminal.

Oslo Rygge Airport (RYG)

Train: Shuttle buses take you to Rygge Station for train connections to Oslo.

Bus: Direct buses operate between the airport and Oslo.

Taxi: Taxis are available but are generally more expensive.

Oslo Torp Airport (TRF)

Train: Shuttle buses connect to Sandefjord Station, from where you can catch a train to Oslo.

Bus: Direct bus services are available.

Taxi: Generally not the preferred option due to cost and distance.

Tips for a Smooth Journey

Check Flight Status: Verify your flight status and any potential delays before heading to the airport.

Arrive Early: Arrive at the airport well in advance of your flight to allow time for check-in, security screening, and other procedures.

Prepare for Security: Follow airport security guidelines by packing liquids and electronics according to regulations.

Local Currency: While credit and debit cards are widely accepted, having a small amount of Norwegian Krone (NOK) for emergencies can be useful.

By Train

Traveling to Oslo by train can be a scenic and relaxing way to reach the Norwegian capital, especially if you're coming from nearby European cities. Here's a comprehensive guide on how to travel to Oslo by train, including routes, services, and tips for a smooth journey.

Major Train Routes to Oslo

From Sweden

Stockholm to Oslo

Route: The train journey from Stockholm, Sweden's capital, to Oslo covers approximately 520 kilometers (320 miles).

Service: SJ (Swedish Railways) operates direct trains on this route, which are comfortable and well-equipped.

Duration: The journey takes about 6 to 7 hours.

Facilities: Onboard facilities include Wi-Fi, power outlets, and food services.

Gothenburg to Oslo

Route: A shorter route from Gothenburg to Oslo, covering around 300 kilometers (186 miles).

Service: SJ offers direct trains on this route, providing a comfortable and efficient service.

Duration: The journey takes about 3.5 to 4 hours.

Facilities: Similar to the Stockholm route, with Wi-Fi and power outlets available.

From Denmark

Copenhagen to Oslo

Route: Traveling from Copenhagen to Oslo typically involves a combination of train and ferry. The journey covers approximately 600 kilometers (373 miles).

Service: You'll take a train from Copenhagen to Malmö, then board a ferry from Helsingborg to Oslo.

Duration: The combined travel time is about 8 to 10 hours, depending on the connection times.

Facilities: Both train and ferry services offer various amenities, including dining options and comfortable seating.

From Norway's Other Cities

Bergen to Oslo

Route: The train from Bergen to Oslo covers approximately 500 kilometers (311 miles).

Service: Vy (Norwegian Railways) operates this scenic route, which is renowned for its stunning landscapes.

Duration: The journey takes about 7 to 8 hours.

Facilities: Onboard amenities include Wi-Fi, food services, and panoramic windows for enjoying the views.

The Ultimate Oslo Travel Guide (2025 Edition)

Stavanger to Oslo

Route: Covering about 300 kilometers (186 miles), this route connects Stavanger with Oslo.

Service: Vy provides a comfortable and efficient train service on this route.

Duration: The journey takes approximately 4 to 5 hours.

Facilities: Features include Wi-Fi, power outlets, and dining options.

Booking Your Train Journey

Tickets and Reservations

Advance Booking: Book tickets in advance to secure the best fares and seat reservations. Tickets can often be purchased up to 3 to 6 months before departure.

Online Booking: Use the websites of rail operators such as SJ (Sweden), Vy (Norway), or international booking platforms like Eurail or Omio to check schedules and book tickets.

Seat Reservations: For popular routes, especially during peak travel seasons, seat reservations are recommended.

Types of Tickets

Standard Class: Offers comfortable seating and basic amenities.

First Class: Provides more spacious seating, enhanced comfort, and additional services.

Flex Tickets: Allow for more flexible travel plans, including changes and cancellations.

Onboard Experience

Comfort and Amenities

Seating: Trains typically offer comfortable seating with ample legroom. First-class tickets provide additional space and comfort.

Wi-Fi: Many trains offer free Wi-Fi, allowing you to stay connected during your journey.

Dining: Onboard dining options vary. Some trains have dining cars or food service, while others allow you to bring your own food and beverages.

Power Outlets: Available on many trains for charging electronic devices.

Scenic Views

Scenic Routes: Particularly on routes such as Bergen to Oslo, you'll experience stunning landscapes, including fjords, mountains, and picturesque countryside.

Panoramic Windows: Most trains have large windows to enhance the viewing experience.

Arrival in Oslo

Oslo Central Station (Oslo S)

Location: Situated in the heart of Oslo, close to major attractions, shopping areas, and public transport.

Facilities: Includes shops, cafes, luggage storage, and ticketing services.

Transportation:

Public Transit: Easy access to buses, trams, and the metro for further travel within Oslo.

Taxis: Available at the station for convenient transport to your accommodation.

Tips for a Smooth Train Journey

Travel Documents

Passports: Carry your passport for international travel and any necessary visas.

Tickets: Keep your tickets and reservations handy, either in print or digitally.

Luggage

Baggage: Most trains have dedicated luggage compartments, but ensure your bags are manageable and comply with any size restrictions.

Valuables: Keep important items like passports, money, and electronics with you at your seat.

Arrive Early

Station Arrival: Arrive at the station a bit earlier than the departure time to find your platform and get settled.

Local Currency

Payment: While many trains accept card payments, having some local currency (Norwegian Krone) for any additional purchases can be useful.

The Ultimate Oslo Travel Guide (2025 Edition)

By Bus

Traveling to Oslo by bus is a cost-effective and straightforward option, particularly for those coming from neighboring countries in Europe. Here's a detailed guide on how to travel to Oslo by bus, including routes, services, tips, and what to expect during your journey.

Major Bus Routes to Oslo

From Sweden

Stockholm to Oslo

Route: Buses travel approximately 520 kilometers (320 miles) from Stockholm to Oslo.

Service: Several companies operate on this route, including FlixBus and Nettbuss (part of Vy). The journey is direct and comfortable.

Duration: The trip typically takes about 8 to 10 hours.

Facilities: Buses usually offer amenities like Wi-Fi, power outlets, air conditioning, and comfortable seating.

Gothenburg to Oslo

Route: This route covers about 300 kilometers (186 miles).

Service: FlixBus and Nettbuss provide direct services between Gothenburg and Oslo.

Duration: The journey takes approximately 4 to 5 hours.

Facilities: Similar amenities to other routes, including Wi-Fi and power outlets.

From Denmark

Copenhagen to Oslo

Route: Traveling from Copenhagen to Oslo by bus involves a combination of bus and ferry. The distance is around 600 kilometers (373 miles).

Service: Companies like FlixBus offer combined bus and ferry tickets.

Duration: The combined travel time is about 8 to 10 hours, including ferry crossing time.

Facilities: Buses offer amenities such as Wi-Fi, power outlets, and comfortable seating. The ferry provides additional comfort and dining options.

From Norway's Other Cities

Bergen to Oslo

Route: The bus journey from Bergen to Oslo covers approximately 500 kilometers (311 miles).

Service: Vy (formerly Nettbuss) operates this route, providing a direct connection.

Duration: The trip takes about 8 to 10 hours.

Facilities: Onboard amenities typically include Wi-Fi, power outlets, and comfortable seating.

Stavanger to Oslo

Route: The distance between Stavanger and Oslo is about 300 kilometers (186 miles).

Service: Vy provides direct bus services on this route.

Duration: The journey takes approximately 5 to 6 hours.

Facilities: Buses are equipped with Wi-Fi, power outlets, and comfortable seats.

Booking Your Bus Journey

Tickets and Reservations

Advance Booking: Book tickets in advance to secure the best fares and seat reservations. Tickets can usually be purchased up to several months before travel.

Online Booking: Use websites or apps of bus operators like FlixBus, Nettbuss, or Vy to check schedules and book tickets.

Ticket Options: Choose from various fare options, including standard and flexible tickets. Some operators also offer discounts for early bookings or group travel.

Types of Tickets

Standard Tickets: Offer basic travel with standard amenities.

Flexible Tickets: Allow for changes or cancellations, providing greater flexibility in your travel plans.

Discounted Tickets: Look for special offers or discounts for students, seniors, or early bookings.

Onboard Experience

Comfort and Amenities

Seating: Buses generally offer comfortable seating with ample legroom. Some operators have premium seating options.

Wi-Fi: Many long-distance buses provide free Wi-Fi to keep you connected during your journey.

Power Outlets: Available on many buses to charge your devices.

Refreshments: Some buses have onboard vending machines or provide access to refreshments. Alternatively, you can bring your own food and drinks.

Scenic Views

Route Scenery: Enjoy picturesque views of the Scandinavian countryside, fjords, and coastal landscapes, particularly on longer routes.

Arrival in Oslo

Oslo Bus Terminal (Oslo Bussterminal)

Location: Situated in the city center, near Oslo Central Station (Oslo S). It's well-connected to public transport and other city amenities.

Facilities: Includes shops, cafes, ticket counters, and information services.

Transportation:

Public Transit: Access to buses, trams, and metro services for further travel within Oslo.

Taxis: Available outside the terminal for convenient transport to your accommodation.

Tips for a Smooth Bus Journey

Travel Documents

Passports: Carry your passport for international travel and any required visas.

Tickets: Keep your bus tickets and reservation details handy, either in print or digitally.

Luggage

Baggage Policy: Check the baggage policy of your bus operator. Most buses allow a certain amount of carry-on and checked luggage.

Valuables: Keep important items like passports, money, and electronics with you at your seat.

Arrive Early

Bus Station Arrival: Arrive at the bus station a bit earlier than the departure time to find your platform and get settled.

Local Currency

Payment: Having some local currency (Norwegian Krone) can be useful for any additional purchases or emergencies.

By Car

Traveling to Oslo by car offers flexibility and the opportunity to enjoy scenic drives through Norway's stunning landscapes. Here's a detailed guide on how to plan and execute a road trip to Oslo, including route options, driving tips, and what to expect upon arrival.

Planning Your Route

From Sweden

Stockholm to Oslo

Route: The drive from Stockholm to Oslo covers about 520 kilometers (320 miles).

Main Route: Take E4 from Stockholm to E20, and then E6 directly to Oslo.

Duration: Approximately 6 to 7 hours, depending on traffic and road conditions.

Scenic Highlights: Enjoy the picturesque landscapes of southern Sweden and the Norwegian countryside.

Gothenburg to Oslo

Route: The drive covers around 300 kilometers (186 miles).

Main Route: Take E6 directly from Gothenburg to Oslo.

Duration: About 3.5 to 4 hours.

Scenic Highlights: Coastal views and charming Swedish towns along the route.

From Denmark

Copenhagen to Oslo

Route: The drive involves a combination of road and ferry. The total distance is around 600 kilometers (373 miles).

Main Route: Drive from Copenhagen to Helsingør, take the ferry to Helsingborg, and then continue on E6 to Oslo.

Duration: Approximately 8 to 10 hours, including ferry crossing time.

Scenic Highlights: The ferry ride offers beautiful views of the Øresund Strait.

From Norway's Other Cities

Bergen to Oslo

Route: The drive covers about 500 kilometers (311 miles).

Main Route: Take E16 from Bergen to Oslo.

Duration: Approximately 7 to 8 hours.

Scenic Highlights: Drive through the mountains and fjords of western Norway.

Stavanger to Oslo

Route: The drive covers around 300 kilometers (186 miles).

Main Route: Take E39 and then E6 directly to Oslo.

Duration: About 4 to 5 hours.

Scenic Highlights: Coastal views and scenic mountain passes.

Preparing for Your Drive

Documentation

Driver's License: Ensure you have a valid driver's license. International Driving Permits (IDP) may be required if your license is not in the Roman alphabet.

Vehicle Registration: Carry your vehicle registration documents.

Insurance: Ensure your car insurance covers driving in Norway. Verify with your insurance provider if additional coverage is needed.

Vehicle Preparation

Check Vehicle: Ensure your car is in good condition, including tires, brakes, and lights. Consider having a pre-trip inspection.

Emergency Kit: Carry an emergency kit that includes a first-aid kit, reflective vest, warning triangle, and basic tools.

Navigation: Use a GPS or navigation app for accurate directions. Offline maps can be useful in areas with poor mobile reception.

Road Rules and Regulations

Speed Limits: Observe speed limits, which are typically 50 km/h (31 mph) in urban areas, 80-90 km/h (50-56 mph) on rural roads, and up to 110 km/h (68 mph) on highways.

Toll Roads: Norway has several toll roads and tunnels. Be prepared for toll charges and check if your rental car includes a toll tag.

Winter Driving: If traveling in winter, ensure your vehicle is equipped with winter tires and carry chains if necessary. Be prepared for snowy and icy conditions.

Headlights: Use dipped headlights at all times, day and night.

Arriving in Oslo

Parking

City Parking: Oslo has various parking options, including street parking and parking garages. Be aware of parking regulations and fees, which can vary by location.

Parking Zones: The city is divided into parking zones with different rates. Use parking meters or apps to pay for parking.

Hotels: Many hotels offer parking facilities. Check with your accommodation to see if parking is included or available at an additional cost.

Traffic and Navigation

Traffic: Oslo's city center can be busy, especially during peak hours. Plan your route and timing to avoid heavy traffic.

Congestion Charge: Oslo has a congestion charge zone for vehicles entering the city center. Be prepared to pay this charge if you plan to drive into the center.

Scenic Drives and Stops

Fjord Landscapes

Norwegian Fjords: If you have time, explore the stunning fjords and coastal scenery along the way. Routes like E16 and E6 offer beautiful views of Norway's natural landscapes.

Historic Towns

Sweden and Denmark: Consider stopping in charming towns and cities along your route, such as Gothenburg or Helsingborg, to break up the journey and enjoy local attractions.

Tips for a Smooth Journey

Plan Ahead

Route Planning: Plan your route, including rest stops and refueling stations.

Accommodation: Book accommodations in advance if you plan to stay overnight during your journey.

Stay Informed

Weather Conditions: Check weather forecasts and road conditions before you depart, especially in winter.

Local Regulations: Familiarize yourself with local driving regulations and road signs.

Local Currency

Payment: While many places accept credit cards, carrying some local currency (Norwegian Krone) can be useful for tolls, parking, and small purchases.

By Ferry

Traveling to Oslo by ferry is a unique and scenic way to arrive in Norway's capital. This method is particularly popular for those coming from Denmark and some other Scandinavian countries. Here's a detailed guide on how to travel to Oslo by ferry, including routes, services, and tips for a smooth journey.

Major Ferry Routes to Oslo

From Denmark

Copenhagen to Oslo

Route: This is the most popular ferry route to Oslo. The journey involves crossing the Øresund Strait and sailing through the Kattegat and Skagerrak straits.

Service Providers: DFDS Seaways operates daily ferries between Copenhagen and Oslo.

Duration: The crossing takes approximately 17 hours.

Facilities: Ferries offer a range of amenities including comfortable cabins, restaurants, bars, shopping, and entertainment options. You can choose between various types of cabins, from basic to luxury.

Helsingør to Oslo

Route: This ferry route connects Helsingør (Elsinore) in Denmark with Helsingborg in Sweden, and then you can drive from Helsingborg to Oslo.

Service Providers: The ferry route between Helsingør and Helsingborg is operated by ForSea Ferries. For the drive from Helsingborg to Oslo, refer to the previous "By Car" guide.

Duration: The ferry ride from Helsingør to Helsingborg takes about 20 minutes. The drive from Helsingborg to Oslo takes around 6 to 7 hours.

Facilities: The ferry offers a range of services, including dining and shopping options.

Booking Your Ferry Journey

Tickets and Reservations

Advance Booking: It's advisable to book your ferry tickets in advance to secure the best fares and availability. Tickets can often be purchased up to several months in advance.

Online Booking: Use ferry operators' websites (like DFDS Seaways) or booking platforms to check schedules and book tickets.

Cabins and Seating: Choose between different cabin options (from basic to deluxe) or opt for a seat in a shared lounge area. Make reservations based on your comfort preferences and budget.

Types of Tickets

Standard Tickets: Include basic travel with access to shared lounges and other general amenities.

Cabin Tickets: Provide a private space for sleeping and additional amenities. Options range from economy to luxury cabins.

Vehicle Tickets: If traveling with a car, you'll need to book a vehicle ticket in addition to passenger tickets. Ensure your vehicle is booked in advance to secure a space.

Onboard Experience

Comfort and Amenities

Accommodation: Choose from various cabin types or lounges. Cabins range from simple to luxurious, providing options for a good night's sleep or a comfortable resting area.

Dining: Enjoy onboard dining options, including restaurants, cafes, and bars. The menu typically features a variety of meals, snacks, and beverages.

Entertainment: Ferries often have entertainment options such as live music, cinemas, and duty-free shops.

Wi-Fi: Some ferries offer Wi-Fi, though it might be subject to an additional fee.

Scenic Views

Ocean Views: Enjoy the beautiful sea views and the changing landscape as you approach Oslo. The ferry ride provides a unique perspective on Scandinavia's coastal beauty.

Arrival in Oslo

Oslo Ferry Terminal

Location: The Oslo Ferry Terminal is located near the city center, making it convenient to access various city attractions and transport options.

Facilities: The terminal has amenities including luggage storage, taxis, and information services.

Transportation:

Public Transit: Easy access to buses, trams, and metro services for further travel within Oslo.

Taxis: Available for convenient transport to your accommodation or other destinations in the city.

Tips for a Smooth Ferry Journey

Travel Documents

Passports: Ensure you have a valid passport for international travel and any necessary visas.

Tickets: Keep your ferry tickets and reservation details handy, either in print or digitally.

Luggage

Baggage Policy: Check the ferry operator's baggage policy. Most ferries allow a certain amount of luggage, but there may be restrictions or fees for excess baggage.

Valuables: Keep important items like passports, money, and electronics with you in your cabin or hand luggage.

Arrival and Disembarkation

Disembarkation: Follow instructions for disembarking, including customs and immigration procedures if required.

Local Currency: Have some Norwegian Krone (NOK) for any immediate expenses or purchases upon arrival.

Weather Conditions

Seasickness: If you're prone to seasickness, consider taking preventative measures such as medication or sea bands. The ferry's movement can be gentle, but it's good to be prepared.

Chapter 4: Getting Around Oslo

Public Transportation

Oslo's public transportation system is well-developed, efficient, and easy to navigate, making it convenient to explore the city. Here's an extensive guide to using Oslo's metro, trams, and buses, including how to plan your trips, understand the fare system, and tips for using public transit in the Norwegian capital.

Oslo Metro (T-Bane)

Overview

Lines: The Oslo Metro, known as T-Bane, consists of five main lines: Line 1 (Furuset), Line 2 (Østerås), Line 3 (Sognsvann), Line 4 (Bryn), and Line 5 (Storo).

Coverage: The metro system covers central Oslo and extends to suburban areas, providing access to key attractions, business districts, and residential neighborhoods.

How to Use

Stations: Metro stations are well-signposted and accessible. Look for the T-Bane symbol (a blue "T").

Frequency: Trains run frequently, with intervals of about 6-15 minutes depending on the time of day and line.

Tickets: Purchase tickets before boarding from vending machines or app. You can use single tickets or a Ruter card for multiple rides.

Key Lines and Stops

Line 1: Connects major stops like Central Station, Grønland, and Furuset.

Line 2: Serves areas including Nationaltheatret and Østerås.

Line 3: Provides access to the University of Oslo (Blindern) and Sognsvann.

Line 4: Runs through the city center, including major stops like St.ortinget.

Line 5: Connects to Storo and Majorstuen.

Oslo Trams

Overview

Lines: Oslo's tram system consists of six main lines: Line 12 (Majorstuen), Line 13 (Bryn), Line 14 (Sognsvann), Line 15 (Grünerløkka), Line 17 (Grefsen), and Line 18 (Tøyen).

Coverage: The tram system covers central Oslo and extends to several neighborhoods, providing a scenic and efficient way to travel.

How to Use

Tram Stops: Look for tram stop signs and schedule boards. Tram stops are marked with a tram icon.

Frequency: Trams run frequently, with intervals of about 10-20 minutes depending on the line and time of day.

Tickets: Purchase tickets before boarding from vending machines or app. The Ruter card can be used for multiple rides.

Key Lines and Stops

Line 12: Serves Majorstuen and parts of the city center.

Line 13: Connects Bryn and central Oslo.

Line 14: Runs through Sognsvann and the city center.

Line 15: Provides access to Grünerløkka and the central area.

Line 17: Connects to Grefsen and parts of the city.

Line 18: Serves Tøyen and the central districts.

Oslo Buses

Overview

Coverage: Oslo's bus system covers the entire city and extends to suburban areas and neighboring towns. Buses complement the metro and tram networks, providing access to locations not covered by rail.

Lines: Buses are numbered based on their routes and can be identified by their destination signs.

How to Use

Bus Stops: Look for bus stop signs with route numbers and schedules. Stops are marked with a bus icon.

Frequency: Buses run frequently, with intervals of about 10-30 minutes depending on the route and time of day.

Tickets: Purchase tickets before boarding from vending machines or app. The Ruter card can be used for multiple rides.

Key Routes and Stops

Bus 30: Connects Majorstuen and Central Station.

Bus 31: Serves the western suburbs and central Oslo.

Bus 34: Runs between parts of central Oslo and the eastern suburbs.

Bus 54: Provides access to various neighborhoods and central Oslo.

Ticketing and Fare System

Types of Tickets

Single Ticket: Valid for one journey on any combination of metro, tram, and bus within the specified fare zones and time limit.

Day Pass: Allows unlimited travel for one day on all public transport within Oslo.

The Ultimate Oslo Travel Guide (2025 Edition)

Ruter Card: A rechargeable smart card that can be loaded with various travel passes or single tickets. It's convenient for frequent travelers and offers discounted fares.

Travel Apps: Use the Ruter app to purchase tickets, check schedules, and plan your trips.

Zones and Fares

Fare Zones: Oslo is divided into fare zones, and ticket prices depend on the number of zones traveled. Most tourists will be traveling within Zone 1, which covers central Oslo.

Payment: Tickets can be purchased at vending machines, online through the Ruter website or app, and at some convenience stores. Contactless payment options are available on some buses and trams.

Accessibility and Tips

Accessibility

Stations and Vehicles: Most metro, tram, and bus stations are equipped with accessibility features such as elevators and ramps. Buses and trams are generally accessible for passengers with mobility issues.

Tips for Using Public Transport

Plan Your Journey: Use the Ruter website or app to plan your routes and check real-time schedules.

Validate Your Ticket: Ensure you validate your ticket or Ruter card before boarding. Some vehicles have onboard ticket validators.

Peak Hours: Public transport can be crowded during rush hours (8-9 AM and 4-6 PM). Plan accordingly if you prefer a quieter journey.

Stay Informed: Pay attention to announcements and display boards for any updates or changes in service.

Renting a Car

Renting a car in Oslo offers flexibility and the opportunity to explore both the city and surrounding areas at your own pace. Here's a comprehensive guide on how to rent a car in Oslo, including tips for choosing a rental, driving in Norway, and making the most of your rental experience.

Choosing a Rental Car

Rental Agencies

International Chains: Major international car rental companies with offices in Oslo include Hertz, Avis, Europcar, Budget, and Sixt.

Local Companies: Local agencies such as Rent-A-Wreck or Oslo Rent a Car offer competitive rates and personalized service.

Types of Cars

Economy: Ideal for city driving and short trips, providing fuel efficiency and ease of parking.

Compact: Suitable for both city driving and longer journeys, with more space than economy cars.

SUVs and Crossovers: Useful for exploring rural areas or traveling in winter conditions.

Luxury: For a more comfortable or stylish experience.

Booking Your Rental

Advance Booking: Book in advance to secure the best rates and availability, especially during peak tourist seasons.

Online Platforms: Use websites or apps of rental companies to compare prices, check car options, and make reservations.

Pick-Up and Drop-Off Locations: Confirm the rental agency's office location, whether it's at the airport or in the city center, and check if they offer pick-up and drop-off services.

Driving in Oslo

Road Rules and Regulations

Speed Limits: Adhere to speed limits: 50 km/h (31 mph) in urban areas, 80-90 km/h (50-56 mph) on rural roads, and up to 110 km/h (68 mph) on highways.

Toll Roads: Norway has toll roads and tunnels, especially in and around Oslo. Be prepared to pay these tolls; some rental companies provide an electronic toll tag.

Winter Driving: If traveling in winter, ensure your rental car is equipped with winter tires. Snow chains may be necessary in snowy conditions.

Parking

City Center Parking: Oslo's city center has various parking options, including street parking and parking garages. Be aware of parking regulations and fees.

Parking Zones: Oslo is divided into parking zones with different rates. Use parking meters or apps to pay.

Hotel Parking: Check with your accommodation to see if they offer parking facilities or if nearby parking options are available.

Traffic and Congestion

Peak Hours: Oslo can experience traffic congestion during rush hours (8-9 AM and 4-6 PM). Plan your routes and travel times accordingly.

Congestion Charge: Oslo has a congestion charge zone for vehicles entering the city center. Be prepared to pay this charge if driving into the center.

Insurance and Coverage

Insurance Options

Basic Insurance: Typically includes liability coverage for damages to other vehicles or property.

Collision Damage Waiver (CDW): Reduces your liability for damage to the rental car, though there may be an excess amount.

Theft Protection: Covers theft of the rental car.

Additional Coverage: Consider additional coverage for peace of mind, such as roadside assistance or personal accident insurance.

Verification

Insurance Check: Verify your insurance coverage with the rental agency and confirm what is included in the rental agreement.

Credit Card Coverage: Check if your credit card offers rental car insurance and if it covers damage or theft.

Picking Up and Returning the Car

Pick-Up

Documentation: Bring your driver's license, credit card, and rental confirmation. International Driving Permits (IDP) may be required if your license is not in the Roman alphabet.

Inspection: Inspect the car for any existing damage before driving off and report any issues to the rental agency.

Instructions: Get instructions on operating the car, including navigation systems, if applicable.

Returning the Car

Fuel: Return the car with a full tank of fuel unless otherwise specified in the rental agreement.

Inspection: Return the car to the agreed location and time. The rental agency will inspect the vehicle for any new damage.

Paperwork: Ensure all paperwork is completed, and obtain a receipt or confirmation of the return.

Tips for Renting a Car in Oslo

Plan Your Routes

Navigation: Use a GPS or navigation app to plan your routes and navigate Oslo and beyond.

Scenic Drives: Explore scenic routes and attractions outside Oslo, such as the Norwegian fjords and picturesque villages.

Emergency Kit

Safety: Carry an emergency kit including a first-aid kit, reflective vest, warning triangle, and basic tools.

Local Laws and Customs

Road Signs: Familiarize yourself with Norwegian road signs and traffic laws.

Driving Etiquette: Follow local driving etiquette and respect speed limits and other regulations.

Weather Conditions

Winter Conditions: Be prepared for winter driving conditions if visiting during the colder months. Check weather forecasts and road conditions before traveling.

Taxis and Ride-Sharing

Navigating Oslo using taxis and ride-sharing services offers convenience and flexibility, particularly if you need door-to-door transport or prefer not to use public transportation. Here's an extensive guide on using taxis and ride-sharing services in Oslo, including how to hail a taxi, use ride-sharing apps, and tips for a smooth experience.

Taxis

Taxi Services

Major Companies: Oslo has several reputable taxi companies, including:

Oslo Taxi: One of the largest taxi services in Oslo, known for its reliability.

NorgesTaxi: A well-established taxi company with extensive coverage in Oslo.

Taxifix: Provides a range of taxi options and services throughout the city.

Hailing a Taxi

Taxi Stands: Taxis can be easily found at designated taxi stands throughout Oslo, especially near major transportation hubs like the Oslo Central Station and the airport.

Phone Booking: You can call a taxi company directly to request a cab. Each company provides a phone number for bookings.

Hail on the Street: Taxis can be hailed on the street if they are displaying an available light. Look for taxis with the "taxi" sign on the roof.

The Ultimate Oslo Travel Guide (2025 Edition)

Taxi Fares

Metered Fares: Fares are generally metered based on distance and time. There may be additional charges for luggage, airport pickups, or late-night services.

Base Fare: Oslo taxis usually have a base fare plus charges per kilometer traveled.

Airport Surcharge: There may be an extra charge for trips to and from Oslo Airport (Gardermoen).

Payment

Methods: Most taxis accept credit/debit cards. Cash payments are also accepted, but it's convenient to use a card.

Tipping: Tipping is not obligatory, but rounding up the fare or leaving a small tip is appreciated.

Taxi Booking Apps

Oslo Taxi App: The official app for Oslo Taxi allows you to book, track, and pay for rides.

NorgesTaxi App: Offers similar features for booking and managing taxi rides.

Ride-Sharing

Popular Ride-Sharing Services

Uber: A well-known global ride-sharing service operating in Oslo. Uber offers various ride options, including standard and premium services.

Bolt: Another popular ride-sharing service available in Oslo, known for competitive pricing and efficient service.

Using Ride-Sharing Apps

Download the App: Install the Uber or Bolt app from the App Store or Google Play Store.

Set Up Your Account: Create an account using your phone number, email, and payment details.

Request a Ride: Open the app, enter your destination, and choose your ride type. The app will match you with a nearby driver.

Track Your Ride: Monitor your driver's location and estimated arrival time on the app.

Payment: Payment is handled through the app, making it cashless and convenient. You can also leave a tip through the app if desired.

Ride-Sharing Fares

Dynamic Pricing: Ride-sharing services often use dynamic pricing, which means fares may vary based on demand, distance, and time of day.

Base Fare: Fares usually include a base rate plus charges for distance and time.

Surge Pricing: Be aware of surge pricing during peak hours or high-demand periods, which can increase the cost of your ride.

Tips for Using Taxis and Ride-Sharing Services

Safety and Comfort

Verify Your Ride: Before getting into a taxi or ride-sharing vehicle, verify the driver's identity and vehicle details against the information provided in the app or on the taxi's signage.

Share Your Trip: Use the app's feature to share your trip details with a friend or family member for added safety.

Language

Communication: Most taxi drivers and ride-sharing drivers in Oslo speak English, but it's helpful to have your destination written down or easily accessible in case of language barriers.

Airport Transfers

Taxi: Taxis are available at Oslo Airport (Gardermoen) and can be hired directly from the airport's taxi stand.

Ride-Sharing: Ride-sharing services also operate from the airport. Follow the instructions in the app for designated pick-up locations.

Local Regulations

Taxi Regulations: Taxis in Oslo are regulated by local authorities, ensuring safety and fair pricing.

Ride-Sharing Rules: Ride-sharing services must comply with local regulations, including insurance requirements and driver background checks.

Booking in Advance

Pre-Book: For airport transfers or trips during peak times, consider pre-booking your taxi or ride-sharing service to ensure availability and avoid long wait times.

Biking in Oslo

Oslo is known for being a bike-friendly city with extensive cycling infrastructure and a commitment to promoting eco-friendly transportation. Biking in Oslo is an excellent way to explore the city, enjoy its parks and waterfronts, and experience its vibrant neighborhoods. Here's a comprehensive guide to biking in Oslo, including bike rental options, popular cycling routes, and tips for a safe and enjoyable ride.

Bike Rental Options

Bike Share Programs

Oslo Bysykkel: The city's bike-sharing system, Oslo Bysykkel, offers an extensive network of bikes available for short-term use.

How to Use: Register online or via the Oslo Bysykkel app to rent a bike. You can pick up and drop off bikes at any of the designated bike stations around the city.

The Ultimate Oslo Travel Guide (2025 Edition)

Pricing: The service offers various payment options, including pay-as-you-go or subscription plans. The first 45 minutes of each ride are usually free, with additional charges for longer rides.

Stations: Bike stations are strategically located throughout Oslo, including key areas such as the city center, major transport hubs, and popular attractions.

Bike Rental Shops

Rent-A-Bike Oslo: Offers a range of rental bikes including city bikes, e-bikes, and mountain bikes. Conveniently located in central Oslo.

Oslo Sportslager: Provides bike rentals along with equipment and accessories. Located near major bike paths and parks.

Nordic Adventure: Specializes in rental bikes for both city riding and outdoor adventures. Offers delivery and pick-up services for added convenience.

Popular Cycling Routes

City Center and Aker Brygge

Route: Explore Oslo's vibrant city center and waterfront areas like Aker Brygge and Tjuvholmen. Enjoy views of the Oslofjord and the modern architecture along the waterfront.

Highlights: Visit attractions such as the Oslo Opera House, Nobel Peace Center, and the Astrup Fearnley Museum.

Frogner Park (Vigeland Park)

Route: Cycle through Frogner Park, home to the famous Vigeland Sculpture Park. The park offers wide paths and beautiful green spaces.

Highlights: See the iconic sculptures by Gustav Vigeland, and enjoy a leisurely ride through the well-maintained park grounds.

Bygdøy Peninsula

Route: Bike to Bygdøy Peninsula, a popular area with several museums and scenic coastal paths.

Highlights: Visit the Viking Ship Museum, the Norwegian Museum of Cultural History, and enjoy the beautiful coastal scenery.

Oslofjord and Akerselva River

Route: Cycle along the Oslofjord and the Akerselva River, which offer picturesque views and recreational paths.

Highlights: Enjoy riverside parks, historic buildings, and natural beauty. The Akerselva path is particularly scenic, passing through green spaces and old industrial sites.

Grünerløkka and Grünerløkka Park

Route: Explore the trendy Grünerløkka neighborhood, known for its vibrant atmosphere, cafes, and street art.

Highlights: Ride through Grünerløkka Park and experience the lively cultural scene of this popular district.

Cycling Infrastructure and Facilities

Bike Lanes and Paths

Dedicated Lanes: Oslo has an extensive network of dedicated bike lanes and paths, making cycling safe and convenient.

Shared Paths: Many paths are shared with pedestrians, so be mindful of others and adhere to local rules.

Bike Parking

Bike Racks: Numerous bike racks are available throughout the city, including at major attractions, shopping areas, and public transport hubs.

Secure Parking: Use designated bike parking areas to ensure the safety of your bike. Some locations offer secure bike parking facilities.

Safety and Regulations

Helmet Use

Helmet Laws: While wearing a helmet is not mandatory for adults, it is strongly recommended for safety. Helmets are required for children under 15.

Cycling Etiquette

Signals: Use hand signals when turning or stopping to alert other road users.

Visibility: Ensure your bike is equipped with front and rear lights, especially if riding in low-light conditions.

Speed Limits: Adhere to speed limits and be cautious in areas with heavy pedestrian traffic.

Road Rules

Traffic Lights: Follow traffic signals and signs. Be aware of bicycle-specific traffic lights in some areas.

Right of Way: Respect the right of way rules and be cautious at intersections and crossings.

Tips for an Enjoyable Ride

Weather Considerations

Rain Gear: Oslo experiences variable weather, so carry rain gear or waterproof clothing to stay comfortable in changing conditions.

Layering: Dress in layers to adjust to fluctuating temperatures during your ride.

Navigation

Maps and Apps: Use maps or cycling apps to plan your routes and find bike-friendly paths. Apps like Google Maps and local cycling apps can help with navigation and route planning.

Bike Maintenance

Check Your Bike: Before setting off, check that your bike is in good condition, including brakes, tires, and gears.

Repair Stations: Look for public bike repair stations or carry a basic repair kit for minor fixes.

Walking Tours

Exploring Oslo on foot allows you to immerse yourself in the city's vibrant culture, historical sites, and scenic beauty. Walking tours provide a flexible and intimate way to experience Oslo's neighborhoods, landmarks, and hidden gems. Here's a comprehensive guide to walking tours in Oslo, including popular routes, self-guided options, and tips for an enjoyable walking experience.

Popular Walking Tour Routes

1. Oslo City Center and Historical Landmarks

Route Highlights

Oslo Opera House: Start your tour at this architectural marvel. Walk up the roof for panoramic views of the city and fjord.

Karl Johans Gate: Stroll down Oslo's main street, lined with shops, cafes, and historic buildings.

Royal Palace: Visit the official residence of the Norwegian monarch and explore the surrounding palace park.

Oslo Cathedral (Oslo Domkirke): Discover Oslo's historic cathedral, known for its beautiful interior and historical significance.

Stortinget: Admire the Norwegian Parliament building and its impressive architecture.

Distance: Approximately 2-3 km (1.2-1.9 miles)

2. Aker Brygge and Tjuvholmen

Route Highlights

Aker Brygge: Wander along this popular waterfront area, known for its restaurants, shops, and vibrant atmosphere.

Tjuvholmen: Explore this modern district with its art galleries, trendy eateries, and beautiful waterfront views.

Astrup Fearnley Museum: Visit this contemporary art museum located at the edge of Tjuvholmen.

Distance: Approximately 2 km (1.2 miles)

3. Frogner Park and Vigeland Sculpture Park

Route Highlights

Frogner Park: Enjoy a leisurely walk through this large urban park, home to the famous Vigeland Sculpture Park.

Vigeland Sculpture Park: Explore over 200 sculptures by Gustav Vigeland, including the iconic Monolith and Sinnataggen.

Distance: Approximately 2.5 km (1.6 miles)

4. Bygdøy Peninsula

Route Highlights

Bygdøy Peninsula: Take a scenic walk around Bygdøy, known for its museums and natural beauty.

Viking Ship Museum: Explore the well-preserved Viking ships and artifacts.

Norwegian Museum of Cultural History: Visit this open-air museum showcasing traditional Norwegian buildings and rural life.

Distance: Approximately 4-5 km (2.5-3.1 miles)

5. Grünerløkka and the Akerselva River

Route Highlights

Grünerløkka: Discover Oslo's trendy district with its vibrant street art, cafes, and shops.

Akerselva River: Walk along the river, enjoying the mix of natural beauty and historical industrial sites.

Nydalen: Continue your walk to see the modern development in the Nydalen area.

Distance: Approximately 3-4 km (1.9-2.5 miles)

Self-Guided Walking Tours

Using Mobile Apps

Oslo Guide: Offers self-guided walking tours with detailed maps and information on local attractions.

GPSmyCity: Provides downloadable walking tour guides with GPS navigation for self-guided tours.

Printed Maps and Guides

Tourist Information Centers: Pick up free maps and walking tour guides from tourist information centers in Oslo.

Local Bookstores: Purchase guidebooks with recommended walking routes and detailed information about Oslo's landmarks.

Tips for an Enjoyable Walking Tour

Comfortable Footwear

Wear Comfortable Shoes: Choose supportive and comfortable walking shoes to enjoy your tour without discomfort.

Weather Preparation

Check the Weather: Oslo's weather can be unpredictable. Dress in layers and carry an umbrella or rain jacket if needed.

Stay Hydrated: Bring a water bottle to stay hydrated during your walk.

Navigation

Use Maps and Apps: Use maps or mobile apps to navigate your route and discover points of interest.

Landmarks and Signage: Follow local landmarks and signage to stay on track and ensure you don't miss key attractions.

Safety and Etiquette

Be Aware of Traffic: Oslo is a pedestrian-friendly city, but be cautious at intersections and crosswalks.

Respect Local Customs: Follow local customs and etiquette, such as being considerate of other pedestrians and respecting quiet zones.

Guided Walking Tours

Tour Companies: Consider joining a guided walking tour for an informative and immersive experience. Some popular options include:

Oslo Walking Tours: Offers themed tours focusing on history, architecture, and culture.

City Walking Tours: Provides guided tours covering various parts of Oslo with local insights.

The Ultimate Oslo Travel Guide (2025 Edition)

Chapter 5: Top Attractions in Oslo

Viking Ship Museum

The Viking Ship Museum is part of the Museum of Cultural History, affiliated with the University of Oslo. It is located on the Bygdøy Peninsula, a picturesque area known for its concentration of museums and beautiful landscapes. The museum houses some of the world's best-preserved Viking ships and a wide array of artifacts that provide invaluable insights into the Viking Age.

History of the Viking Ship Museum

The Viking Ship Museum was established to house and display three Viking ships discovered in burial mounds in southern Norway. These ships were unearthed during the late 19th and early 20th centuries and were remarkably well-preserved due to the clay soil in which they were buried. The museum building itself, designed by architect Arnstein Arneberg, was opened in 1926 and later expanded to accommodate the growing collection.

Key Historical Points

Gokstad Ship (discovered in 1880): Found in a burial mound at Gokstad in Sandefjord, this ship dates back to around 890 AD. It is one of the best-preserved Viking ships ever discovered.

Oseberg Ship (discovered in 1904): Unearthed in a large burial mound at the Oseberg farm near Tønsberg, this ship dates to approximately 834 AD. It is renowned for its ornate carvings and artifacts.

The Ultimate Oslo Travel Guide (2025 Edition)

Tune Ship (discovered in 1867): The first Viking ship ever discovered, found in a burial mound at the Haugen farm in Østfold, dating back to around 900 AD.

Exhibits and Collections

Viking Ships

Oseberg Ship: The centerpiece of the museum, this ship is notable for its elaborate decoration and craftsmanship. It was used as a burial ship for two prominent women, and its excavation revealed a wealth of grave goods, including textiles, household items, and carved wooden artifacts.

Gokstad Ship: A larger and more robust vessel than the Oseberg Ship, it is believed to have been a seagoing vessel capable of long voyages. The burial mound contained the remains of a Viking chieftain and various items, including weapons and a game board.

Tune Ship: Although less complete than the other two ships, the Tune Ship provides important insights into Viking shipbuilding techniques and burial customs.

Artifacts

Grave Goods: The museum displays numerous artifacts recovered from the burial mounds, including sledges, carts, textiles, and everyday items that shed light on Viking life and society.

Wooden Carvings: Intricately carved wooden objects from the Oseberg find, showcasing the artistic skills of the Vikings.

Tools and Equipment: Various tools, weapons, and navigational instruments used by the Vikings.

Location

The Viking Ship Museum is situated on the Bygdøy Peninsula, a short distance from central Oslo. The address is: Huk Aveny 35, 0287 Oslo, Norway

Opening and Closing Hours

Summer Season (May to September): Open daily from 9:00 AM to 6:00 PM

Winter Season (October to April): Open daily from 10:00 AM to 4:00 PM

Closed: Some public holidays, so it's advisable to check the museum's official website for exact dates and times.

Visitor Information

Admission Fees

Adults: NOK 120

Students/Seniors: NOK 90

Children (6-17 years): NOK 50

Family Ticket (2 adults + children): NOK 300

Children under 6: Free

Facilities

Restrooms: Available on-site.

Café: Light refreshments and snacks available.

Gift Shop: Offers a variety of Viking-themed souvenirs and books.

Accessibility

The museum is wheelchair accessible, with ramps and elevators available for visitors with mobility impairments.

Things to Do

Guided Tours

Audio Guides: Available in multiple languages, providing detailed information about the exhibits.

Group Tours: Can be arranged in advance, offering an in-depth exploration of the museum's collections.

Special Exhibitions

The museum occasionally hosts special exhibitions that delve deeper into specific aspects of Viking culture and history.

Educational Programs

Workshops and Lectures: The museum offers various educational programs, including workshops, lectures, and activities for children.

Exploring Bygdøy

Other Museums: Visit nearby attractions such as the Norwegian Museum of Cultural History, the Fram Museum, and the Kon-Tiki Museum.

Outdoor Activities: Enjoy the scenic beauty of Bygdøy with walking trails and beaches.

Tips for Visiting

Arrive Early: To avoid crowds and have a more leisurely experience, try to arrive early in the morning, especially during peak tourist season.

Use Public Transportation: Bygdøy can be easily reached by bus or ferry from central Oslo. The ferry ride offers beautiful views of the Oslofjord.

Plan Ahead: Check the museum's website for any special events or temporary exhibitions that might be of interest.

Dress Comfortably: Wear comfortable shoes and dress appropriately for the weather, as there's a fair amount of walking involved.

Photography: Photography is allowed, but flash is prohibited to protect the artifacts.

Stay Informed: Take advantage of the audio guides and informational plaques to fully appreciate the history and significance of the exhibits.

Oslo Opera House

The Oslo Opera House, located in the Bjørvika district at the edge of the Oslofjord, is the home of the Norwegian National Opera and Ballet. It is renowned for its modern design, which allows visitors to walk on its roof and enjoy panoramic views of the city and the fjord. The building serves as a hub for cultural activities, performances, and architectural admiration.

History

Planning and Construction

Concept and Design: The idea for a new opera house in Oslo was first proposed in the late 1990s. In 2000, the Norwegian government decided to build the new opera house, and an architectural competition was held.

Architects: The Norwegian architecture firm Snøhetta won the competition with their innovative design that integrates the building with its surroundings, creating a seamless transition between land and water.

Construction Timeline: Construction began in 2003 and was completed in 2007. The opera house was officially opened by King Harald V on April 12, 2008.

Significance

The Oslo Opera House quickly became a symbol of contemporary Norwegian architecture and a major cultural venue. It has received numerous awards and accolades for its design and has attracted millions of visitors from around the world.

Architectural Features

Exterior Design

White Marble and Granite: The building's exterior is clad in Italian white marble and granite, giving it a striking, luminous appearance.

Sloping Roof: One of the most distinctive features of the opera house is its sloping roof, which visitors can walk on. The roof slopes gently from the ground level up to the peak, offering an inviting public space.

Glass Facade: The large glass facade facing the fjord provides stunning views and creates a sense of openness and transparency.

Interior Design

Main Auditorium: The main auditorium, with a seating capacity of 1,364, features oak paneling and excellent acoustics, designed to enhance the audience's experience.

Secondary Stages: In addition to the main stage, the opera house includes smaller stages for more intimate performances.

Public Spaces: The interior also includes several public spaces, such as the foyer, which offers views of the fjord and the city.

Performances and Events

Opera and Ballet

The Oslo Opera House hosts a wide range of performances, including operas, ballets, and concerts. The Norwegian National Opera and Ballet, the resident company, presents both classic and contemporary works.

Concerts and Recitals

In addition to opera and ballet, the venue also hosts concerts, recitals, and other musical events, featuring both Norwegian and international artists.

Special Events

The opera house frequently holds special events, such as festivals, premieres, and cultural celebrations, making it a vibrant hub of activity throughout the year.

Location

The Oslo Opera House is located in the Bjørvika district, at Kirsten Flagstads Plass 1, 0150 Oslo, Norway. It is easily accessible by public transportation, including buses, trams, and trains, with the Oslo Central Station (Oslo S) nearby.

Opening and Closing Hours

Box Office: Typically open from 11:00 AM to 6:00 PM on weekdays, with extended hours on performance days.

Public Areas: The roof and public spaces are generally open to visitors from early morning until late evening, but it's advisable to check the official website for current hours and any special closures.

Visitor Information

Admission

Public Access: Access to the roof and public areas is free of charge.

Performance Tickets: Prices for performances vary depending on the production and seating. Tickets can be purchased online, at the box office, or through authorized vendors.

Guided Tours

Architectural Tours: The opera house offers guided tours that provide insights into the building's design, construction, and cultural significance. These tours are available in multiple languages.

Backstage Tours: For a behind-the-scenes look, consider booking a backstage tour to see the production areas and learn about the workings of the opera house.

Facilities

Café and Restaurant: Enjoy a meal or refreshment at the opera house's café and restaurant, which offer a range of dining options with beautiful views.

Gift Shop: The on-site gift shop offers souvenirs, books, and other items related to the opera house and its performances.

Things to Do

Walking on the Roof

One of the unique experiences offered by the Oslo Opera House is the ability to walk on its roof. The sloping design provides a gentle ascent to the top, where you can enjoy panoramic views of the Oslofjord, the city skyline, and the surrounding areas.

Exploring Bjørvika

Barcode Project: Nearby, the Barcode Project is a series of modern high-rise buildings with interesting architecture. It's worth a stroll to see the contrast between the opera house and these contemporary structures.

Sørenga: Just a short walk away, the Sørenga district offers swimming spots and more dining options along the waterfront.

Photography

The opera house is a popular spot for photography, offering numerous angles and perspectives for capturing its architectural beauty. Sunrise and sunset are particularly good times for photos.

Tips for Visiting

Book Tickets in Advance: For performances, it's best to book tickets well in advance, especially for popular shows.

Check the Schedule: Look at the opera house's official website to see what performances and events are scheduled during your visit.

Wear Comfortable Shoes: If you plan to walk on the roof, wear comfortable shoes with good grip, as the marble surface can be slippery, especially when wet.

Explore the Surroundings: Take some time to explore the Bjørvika district and nearby attractions for a fuller experience.

Join a Tour: Enhance your visit by joining an architectural or backstage tour to gain deeper insights into the opera house's design and operations.

Dining Options: Plan a meal at the on-site restaurant to enjoy the views and a relaxed dining experience.

Akershus Fortress

Akershus Fortress is a medieval castle that has played a crucial role in Norway's history. It served as a royal residence, military stronghold, and government center over the centuries. Today, it is a popular tourist attraction, offering a blend of historical exploration, scenic views, and cultural experiences.

History of Akershus Fortress

Origins and Construction

Early Beginnings: The fortress was founded in the late 13th century by King Håkon V as a defensive structure to protect Oslo. The original castle was constructed on a hill overlooking the Oslofjord, chosen for its strategic location.

Expansion and Fortification: Over the centuries, the fortress was expanded and fortified by various rulers. Notable additions include the Gothic-style Rosenkrantz Tower, which was built in the 16th century by King Frederik II.

Role and Significance

Royal Residence: Akershus Fortress served as a royal residence during the medieval period and into the Renaissance. It housed Norwegian monarchs and their courts.

Military Importance: The fortress played a crucial role in defending Oslo from various military threats, including Swedish invasions and World War II occupation.

Government Use: In the 19th and early 20th centuries, the fortress was used as a government building and military headquarters.

Modern Era

Restoration: After World War II, the fortress underwent significant restoration and preservation efforts to maintain its historical integrity.

Museum and Visitor Center: Today, Akershus Fortress is a museum and a popular tourist attraction, offering guided tours and exhibits about its history and significance.

Exhibits and Attractions

Rosenkrantz Tower

Architecture and History: The Rosenkrantz Tower is one of the most prominent features of the fortress. Built by King Frederik II in the 16th century, it is a prime example of Renaissance military architecture.

Interior: Visitors can explore the tower's interior, which includes period rooms, a chapel, and an impressive view from the top.

The Castle Courtyard

Historic Buildings: The castle courtyard is surrounded by several historic buildings, including the medieval King's Hall and various barracks.

Scenic Views: The courtyard offers stunning views of the Oslofjord and the city, making it a popular spot for photographs.

The Norwegian Armed Forces Museum

Exhibits: The museum showcases Norway's military history, with exhibits on weapons, uniforms, and military equipment from various periods.

Interactive Displays: It includes interactive displays and educational information about Norway's military heritage.

The Resistance Museum

World War II Focus: This museum is dedicated to Norway's resistance movement during World War II. It offers insights into the bravery and struggles of Norwegians who fought against Nazi occupation.

Artifacts and Stories: Visitors can see artifacts, photographs, and hear stories of resistance fighters.

The Akershus Festning Restaurant

Dining: The fortress houses a restaurant that offers traditional Norwegian cuisine in a historic setting. It's a great place to enjoy a meal with views of the Oslofjord.

Location

Akershus Fortress is situated in the city center of Oslo, near the Oslo City Hall and the waterfront. The address is: Akershus Festning, 0150 Oslo, Norway

Opening and Closing Hours

Summer Season (May to September): Open daily from 6:00 AM to 9:00 PM.

Winter Season (October to April): Open daily from 6:00 AM to 8:00 PM.

Museums and Exhibits: The Norwegian Armed Forces Museum and the Resistance Museum typically open from 10:00 AM to 4:00 PM, with extended hours during peak tourist season.

Closed: Some public holidays and for special events, so it's advisable to check the official website for the latest information.

Visitor Information

Admission Fees

Fortress Grounds: Access to the fortress grounds is generally free of charge.

Museums: Entrance fees for the Norwegian Armed Forces Museum and the Resistance Museum may apply. It's best to check their websites for current prices.

Facilities

Restrooms: Available within the fortress complex.

Café and Restaurant: The Akershus Festning Restaurant offers dining options with views.

Gift Shop: There is a gift shop where visitors can purchase souvenirs and books related to the fortress and Norwegian history.

Things to Do

Guided Tours

Historical Tours: Join a guided tour to learn about the fortress's history, architecture, and significance. Tours are available in multiple languages and offer in-depth information.

Themed Tours: Special themed tours may be available, focusing on specific aspects of the fortress's history or its role in World War II.

Exploring the Grounds

Walking Tours: Explore the fortress grounds on your own or join a walking tour to discover its hidden corners and historical details.

Photography: The fortress provides excellent opportunities for photography, with its historic architecture and scenic views.

Educational Programs

Workshops and Events: The fortress occasionally hosts workshops, lectures, and events related to Norwegian history and military heritage.

Tips for Visiting

Wear Comfortable Shoes: The fortress grounds are large and include cobblestone paths and uneven surfaces, so comfortable walking shoes are recommended.

Check the Weather: Oslo's weather can be unpredictable, so dress in layers and bring a rain jacket if necessary.

Visit Early: Arriving early can help you avoid crowds and give you more time to explore the various attractions.

Guided Tours: Consider joining a guided tour for a deeper understanding of the fortress's history and significance.

Photography: Take advantage of the scenic views and historical architecture for memorable photos.

Check for Events: Look up any special events or temporary exhibitions before your visit to make the most of your experience.

Vigeland Park (Frogner Park)

Vigeland Park, located within Frogner Park, is the world's largest sculpture park made by a single artist. The park features more than 200 bronze, granite, and cast iron sculptures created by Norwegian sculptor Gustav Vigeland. Open to the public year-round, Vigeland Park attracts over a million visitors annually who come to admire the unique and often thought-provoking sculptures that explore the human condition.

History of Vigeland Park

Gustav Vigeland's Vision

Early Beginnings: Gustav Vigeland (1869-1943) began his ambitious project in the 1920s. He was granted a new studio in exchange for his artworks being donated to the city of Oslo.

Development: Vigeland spent the next two decades designing and creating the sculptures and the architectural layout of the park. His work was driven by themes of life, death, and the human experience.

Completion: Although Vigeland died in 1943, his work was completed according to his designs. The park opened to the public in its current form in the early 1950s.

Notable Sculptures and Features

The Monolith (Monolitten)

Description: The Monolith is the central piece of Vigeland Park, standing at 14 meters tall and carved from a single block of granite. It depicts 121 human figures intertwined and reaching upwards, symbolizing the struggle and beauty of life.

Location: At the highest point in the park, the Monolith is surrounded by a platform with additional sculptures.

The Wheel of Life (Livshjulet)

Description: This sculpture represents the eternal cycle of life, with intertwined human figures forming a circle. It is one of the last works completed by Vigeland.

Symbolism: The Wheel of Life symbolizes eternity and the continuum of human existence.

The Angry Boy (Sinnataggen)

Description: One of the most famous sculptures in the park, The Angry Boy depicts a young boy in a moment of temper, captured with vivid realism and emotion.

Popularity: It is a favorite among visitors, often seen posing with the sculpture.

The Bridge (Broen)

Description: The bridge is adorned with 58 bronze sculptures that depict people in various stages of life and emotional states. It is one of the park's most visited areas.

Themes: The sculptures on the bridge explore relationships, play, and the complexities of human emotions.

The Fountain (Fontenen)

Description: The fountain is surrounded by a series of bronze reliefs that illustrate the cycle of life from birth to death. The central basin is supported by six giant men holding a large bowl.

Interpretation: The fountain represents life's journey and the passage of time.

Location

Vigeland Park is situated within Frogner Park in Oslo's Frogner borough. The address is: Nobels gate 32, 0268 Oslo, Norway

Opening and Closing Hours

Park Grounds: Open 24 hours a day, year-round.

Visitor Center: Typically open from 10:00 AM to 6:00 PM in the summer months, with shorter hours in the winter.

Visitor Information

Admission

Free Entry: Both Vigeland Park and Frogner Park are free to enter and explore.

Facilities

Restrooms: Available near the main entrances and within the park.

Café: There is a café in the park where visitors can enjoy light refreshments.

Gift Shop: The visitor center includes a gift shop with souvenirs and books about Vigeland's work.

Accessibility

Paths: The park is wheelchair accessible, with paved paths and ramps in most areas.

Seating: Benches are available throughout the park for resting and enjoying the scenery.

Things to Do

Guided Tours

Historical and Art Tours: Join a guided tour to learn about the history of the park and the meaning behind Vigeland's sculptures. Tours are available in multiple languages.

Self-Guided Tours: Informational plaques and brochures are available for those who prefer to explore at their own pace.

Photography

Iconic Views: Vigeland Park offers numerous opportunities for photography, with its dramatic sculptures and beautiful landscape. Early morning and late afternoon provide the best light.

Seasonal Activities

Summer: The park is particularly vibrant in the summer, with lush greenery and various outdoor events and festivals.

Winter: In winter, the park is quieter but equally enchanting, with the sculptures often covered in snow, creating a serene atmosphere.

Tips for Visiting

Plan Your Visit: Allocate at least a couple of hours to fully explore the park and appreciate the sculptures.

Dress Comfortably: Wear comfortable shoes and dress appropriately for the weather, as there is a lot of walking involved.

Bring a Camera: The park's sculptures and landscapes are perfect for photography, so don't forget your camera.

Pack a Picnic: Consider bringing a picnic to enjoy in the beautiful surroundings. There are plenty of spots to sit and relax.

Check for Events: Look up any special events or guided tours happening during your visit to enhance your experience.

Respect the Art: While the sculptures are meant to be interactive, be mindful and respectful of the art and other visitors.

Munch Museum

The Munch Museum houses the largest collection of Edvard Munch's art, including over 28,000 works comprising paintings, prints, drawings, sculptures, and photographs. The museum not only showcases Munch's masterpieces but also explores his influence on contemporary art and his enduring legacy.

History of the Munch Museum

Origins and Development

Founding: The Munch Museum was founded in 1963 to mark the 100th anniversary of Edvard Munch's birth. The museum was established based on Munch's own wishes, as he donated all his remaining works to the city of Oslo upon his death in 1944.

Expansion: In 2021, a new, state-of-the-art Munch Museum opened in the Bjørvika district, near the Oslo Opera House. This modern facility offers expansive gallery spaces, advanced conservation areas, and enhanced visitor amenities.

Significance

The Munch Museum serves as a cultural hub, preserving and promoting the works of Edvard Munch. It plays a crucial role in art education and appreciation, offering a deep dive into Munch's artistic evolution and impact.

Collections and Exhibits

Permanent Collection

The Scream: The museum houses several versions of Munch's most famous work, "The Scream," including paintings and lithographs. This iconic piece is a highlight for many visitors.

Madonna: Another of Munch's renowned works, "Madonna," is prominently displayed, exemplifying his unique style and thematic focus on life, death, and love.

The Frieze of Life: This series of paintings explores themes of love, anxiety, and death, reflecting Munch's philosophical and emotional preoccupations.

Self-Portraits: Munch's numerous self-portraits offer insight into his personal struggles and artistic journey.

Special Exhibits

The museum regularly hosts temporary exhibitions that explore various aspects of Munch's work, his contemporaries, and his influence on modern and contemporary art. These exhibits often include loans from other prestigious institutions and feature multimedia presentations.

Photography and Personal Items

In addition to his artworks, the museum displays photographs and personal items that provide a deeper understanding of Munch's life, including his relationships, travels, and artistic process.

Location

The Munch Museum is located in the Bjørvika district of Oslo, at: Edvard Munchs Plass 1, 0194 Oslo, Norway

Opening and Closing Hours

Regular Hours: The museum is generally open from 10:00 AM to 6:00 PM daily.

Extended Hours: On Thursdays, the museum often extends its hours until 9:00 PM.

Closed: Some public holidays and special occasions, so it's best to check the official website for up-to-date information.

Visitor Information

Admission Fees

General Admission: There is an entry fee for adults, with discounts available for seniors, students, and children.

Free Days: The museum occasionally offers free admission days, especially for certain groups like students or Oslo residents.

Facilities

Café and Restaurant: The museum features a café and a restaurant with views of the Oslofjord, offering a range of dining options from light snacks to full meals.

Gift Shop: The on-site gift shop sells a variety of Munch-themed merchandise, including prints, books, and souvenirs.

Accessibility: The museum is fully accessible to visitors with disabilities, with elevators and ramps available.

Guided Tours

Daily Tours: The museum offers daily guided tours in multiple languages, providing in-depth insights into Munch's works and themes.

Private Tours: Private tours can be arranged for groups, offering a more personalized experience.

Things to Do

Explore the Galleries

Spend time exploring the various galleries to fully appreciate Munch's artistic range and evolution. Pay special attention to his use of color, symbolism, and emotional intensity.

Participate in Workshops

The museum offers workshops and educational programs for visitors of all ages, focusing on Munch's techniques and themes. These activities provide a hands-on way to engage with his art.

Attend Special Events

The museum frequently hosts special events, including lectures, film screenings, and performances, that delve deeper into Munch's life and legacy. Check the museum's calendar for upcoming events.

Enjoy the Views

The new Munch Museum's location offers stunning views of the Oslofjord and the city. Take some time to enjoy the scenery from the museum's viewing areas.

Tips for Visiting

Buy Tickets in Advance: Purchase tickets online in advance to avoid long queues, especially during peak tourist season.

Plan Your Visit: Allocate at least two to three hours to fully explore the museum and participate in any tours or workshops.

Check the Schedule: Look at the museum's event schedule to see if there are any special exhibitions or events during your visit.

Use the Audio Guide: Make use of the museum's audio guide for detailed explanations of key works and themes.

Combine Visits: Consider combining your visit to the Munch Museum with a trip to the nearby Oslo Opera House or the Barcode Project for a full day of cultural experiences.

Respect the Art: While photography without flash is usually allowed, be respectful of the artwork and other visitors by following museum guidelines.

The Norwegian Museum of Cultural History (Norsk Folkemuseum)

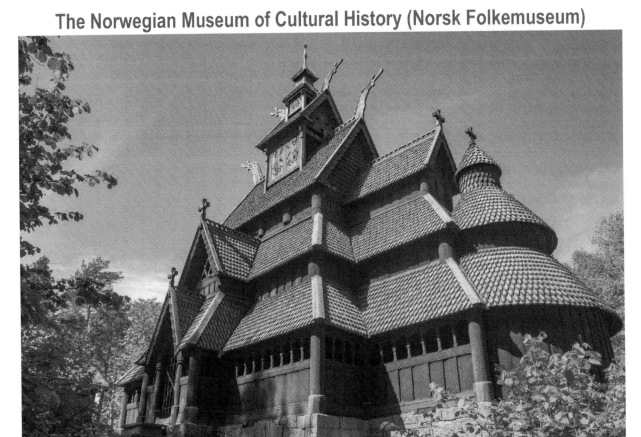

The Norsk Folkemuseum is an open-air museum situated on the Bygdøy Peninsula in Oslo. It features over 160 historic buildings relocated from different parts of Norway, providing a vivid portrayal of Norwegian life from the Middle Ages to the 20th century. The museum also includes indoor exhibits that showcase traditional Norwegian folk art, costumes, and everyday items.

History of the Norsk Folkemuseum

Founding and Development

Establishment: The Norsk Folkemuseum was founded in 1894 by Hans Aall, who aimed to preserve Norway's cultural history and traditions during a time of rapid modernization and industrialization.

Expansion: Over the decades, the museum expanded its collection and relocated numerous historic buildings to its site on Bygdøy, creating an immersive and comprehensive representation of Norwegian heritage.

Modernization: The museum has continued to evolve, incorporating modern technologies and interactive exhibits to enhance the visitor experience while maintaining its focus on historical preservation.

Collections and Exhibits

Open-Air Museum

Historic Buildings: The open-air section features a wide variety of buildings, including farmhouses, barns, stables, and churches, from different regions and time periods. Notable structures include the Gol Stave Church, a stunning 13th-century wooden church, and traditional Sami dwellings.

Period Interiors: Many buildings are furnished with period-appropriate interiors, providing insight into the daily lives of Norwegians across different eras. Guides often dress in traditional costumes, offering demonstrations and stories about life in historical Norway.

Thematic Areas: The open-air museum is divided into several thematic areas, each representing a different region or aspect of Norwegian culture, such as coastal communities, rural life, and urban developments.

Indoor Exhibits

Folk Art and Costumes: The museum's indoor galleries feature extensive collections of Norwegian folk art, including wood carvings, textiles, and rosemaling (decorative painting). Traditional costumes from various regions, known as bunads, are also on display.

Everyday Life: Exhibits explore everyday life in Norway through different historical periods, showcasing household items, tools, toys, and other artifacts that provide a window into the past.

Seasonal Exhibitions: The museum hosts temporary exhibitions that focus on specific aspects of Norwegian culture, history, and contemporary issues, often drawing on its rich collection.

Special Programs

Living History: During the summer months and on special occasions, the museum offers living history programs where actors portray historical characters, bringing the past to life through interactive performances and demonstrations.

Workshops and Activities: Visitors can participate in traditional crafts, cooking demonstrations, and other hands-on activities that highlight Norwegian cultural traditions.

Location

The Norsk Folkemuseum is located on the scenic Bygdøy Peninsula, which is also home to several other major museums. The address is: Museumsveien 10, 0287 Oslo, Norway

Opening and Closing Hours

Summer Season (May to September): Open daily from 10:00 AM to 6:00 PM.

Winter Season (October to April): Open daily from 11:00 AM to 4:00 PM.

Special Hours: The museum may have extended hours during holidays or for special events, so it's advisable to check the official website for the latest information.

Visitor Information

Admission Fees

General Admission: There is an entry fee for adults, with discounts available for seniors, students, and children. Family tickets and annual passes are also available.

Free Days: The museum occasionally offers free admission days or reduced rates for certain groups, such as Oslo residents or students.

Facilities

Restrooms: Available throughout the museum grounds.

Café and Restaurant: The museum features a café and a restaurant that offer traditional Norwegian dishes and refreshments.

Gift Shop: The on-site gift shop sells a variety of Norwegian crafts, books, and souvenirs related to the museum's exhibits.

Accessibility

Paths and Ramps: The museum is largely accessible to visitors with disabilities, with paved paths and ramps in most areas. Some historic buildings may have limited accessibility due to their age and construction.

Guided Tours: Special tours can be arranged for visitors with mobility issues or other needs.

Things to Do

Explore the Open-Air Museum

Guided Tours: Join a guided tour to learn about the history and significance of the various buildings and exhibits. Tours are available in multiple languages and offer in-depth insights.

Self-Guided Tours: Informational plaques and brochures are available for those who prefer to explore at their own pace. Audio guides may also be available.

Interactive Demonstrations: During the summer, participate in traditional activities such as blacksmithing, baking, and textile crafts.

Visit the Indoor Exhibits

Art and Costumes: Spend time in the indoor galleries to appreciate the intricate details of Norwegian folk art and the beauty of traditional costumes.

Temporary Exhibitions: Check out the museum's temporary exhibitions, which provide fresh perspectives and new topics for exploration.

Seasonal Activities and Events

Holiday Celebrations: The museum hosts special events during holidays such as Christmas and Easter, featuring traditional decorations, markets, and activities.

Cultural Festivals: Attend festivals and cultural events that celebrate various aspects of Norwegian heritage, including music, dance, and cuisine.

Tips for Visiting

Wear Comfortable Shoes: The museum grounds are extensive, and there is a lot of walking involved. Comfortable shoes are recommended.

Check the Weather: Dress appropriately for the weather, as much of the museum is outdoors. Bring rain gear or sun protection as needed.

Plan Your Visit: Allocate at least half a day to explore the museum thoroughly. Consider spending a full day if you want to participate in activities and visit nearby attractions on Bygdøy Peninsula.

Bring a Camera: The historic buildings and scenic grounds provide excellent photo opportunities.

Pack a Picnic: There are several picnic areas where you can enjoy a meal amidst the beautiful surroundings.

Explore Nearby Attractions: Combine your visit to the Norsk Folkemuseum with other nearby museums, such as the Viking Ship Museum or the Fram Museum, for a full day of cultural exploration.

Holmenkollen Ski Jump

Holmenkollen Ski Jump is a state-of-the-art ski jumping hill located in the Holmenkollen neighborhood of Oslo. The facility is part of the Holmenkollen National Arena, which also includes cross-country skiing tracks and a biathlon stadium. The ski jump is renowned for its sleek, modern design and serves as a venue for international ski competitions, including the annual Holmenkollen Ski Festival.

History of the Holmenkollen Ski Jump

Early Beginnings

First Competition: The first ski jumping competition at Holmenkollen was held in 1892, making it one of the oldest ski jumping venues in the world.

Development: Over the years, the ski jump has undergone several renovations and reconstructions to meet the evolving standards of the sport and to improve spectator facilities.

Modern Era

2011 Reconstruction: The most significant recent redevelopment was completed in 2011, transforming the ski jump into a modern architectural marvel. Designed by JDS Architects, the new structure is made of steel and concrete and features a distinctive curving profile.

Milestones: The new Holmenkollen Ski Jump has hosted numerous prestigious events, including the FIS Nordic World Ski Championships and World Cup competitions.

Facilities and Attractions

Ski Jump Tower

Observation Deck: The ski jump tower features an observation deck at the top, offering breathtaking panoramic views of Oslo, the Oslofjord, and the surrounding forests.

Museum: Inside the tower, the Holmenkollen Ski Museum provides an in-depth look at the history of skiing, with exhibits on polar expeditions, modern skiing equipment, and the development of ski jumping.

Ski Simulator

Experience the Jump: Visitors can try the ski simulator, which gives a realistic sense of what it's like to fly down the Holmenkollen Ski Jump. It's an exciting experience for both kids and adults.

Holmenkollen Chapel

Historic Site: Nearby, the Holmenkollen Chapel, originally built in 1913 and rebuilt after a fire in 1992, is a picturesque wooden church that adds to the cultural atmosphere of the area.

Location

Holmenkollen Ski Jump is located in the Holmenkollen neighborhood of Oslo, easily accessible by public transportation or car. The address is: Kongeveien 5, 0787 Oslo, Norway

Opening and Closing Hours

Ski Museum and Tower: Generally open daily from 10:00 AM to 4:00 PM, with extended hours in the summer months.

Ski Simulator: Open during museum hours, though it's advisable to check for any seasonal variations or special event closures.

Visitor Information

Admission Fees

General Admission: There is an entry fee for adults, with discounts available for seniors, students, and children. Combined tickets for the ski jump tower, museum, and ski simulator are also available.

Family Tickets: Special family tickets and group rates can provide additional savings.

Facilities

Café and Restaurant: The on-site café offers refreshments and light meals, with stunning views over Oslo.

Gift Shop: The gift shop sells a range of souvenirs, including ski-themed items and Norwegian crafts.

Restrooms: Available within the museum and near the observation deck.

Accessibility

Elevators: Elevators are available to take visitors to the top of the ski jump tower, making it accessible to those with mobility issues.

Paths: The surrounding area has well-maintained paths, though some steep sections may require assistance.

Things to Do

Explore the Ski Museum

Historical Exhibits: Spend time in the Holmenkollen Ski Museum, which showcases over 4,000 years of skiing history and offers fascinating insights into Norway's skiing culture.

Enjoy the Views

Observation Deck: Take in the stunning 360-degree views from the top of the ski jump tower. Clear days offer the best visibility, so check the weather forecast before your visit.

Try the Ski Simulator

Thrill Ride: Experience the adrenaline rush of ski jumping without leaving the ground by trying out the ski simulator. It's a fun and educational activity for all ages.

Attend Events

Ski Competitions: If you visit during winter, you might catch a ski jumping competition or the annual Holmenkollen Ski Festival, which features world-class athletes and vibrant festivities.

Hiking and Nature Walks

Nearby Trails: The area around Holmenkollen offers excellent hiking trails and nature walks. Explore the beautiful Nordmarka forest and enjoy outdoor activities year-round.

Tips for Visiting

Check Event Schedules: If you're interested in watching a ski jumping event, check the schedule in advance to plan your visit around competition dates.

Dress Appropriately: The top of the ski jump can be windy and cold, even in summer. Dress in layers and bring a windbreaker.

Combine with Other Attractions: Holmenkollen is close to other attractions like the Norwegian Museum of Cultural History and the Viking Ship Museum. Consider combining visits to make the most of your day.

Use Public Transport: The Holmenkollen Metro Station (Line 1) provides easy access to the ski jump. The metro ride offers scenic views and is an experience in itself.

Arrive Early: To avoid crowds, especially during peak tourist season, try to arrive early in the day.

Bring a Camera: The views from the observation deck are spectacular and perfect for photography.

Fram Museum

The Fram Museum showcases the achievements of Norwegian polar explorers, focusing on the Fram, a ship renowned for its polar expeditions. The museum offers a deep dive into the harsh environments of the Arctic and Antarctic, the remarkable journeys of explorers like Fridtjof Nansen and Roald Amundsen, and the innovations that made these expeditions possible.

History of the Fram Museum

Origins and Development

Establishment: The Fram Museum was founded in 1936 to preserve the Fram and the legacy of Norwegian polar exploration. The museum was established by the Norwegian Polar Institute and dedicated to educating the public about the heroic age of exploration.

Expansion: Over the years, the museum has expanded its exhibits and facilities, continually updating its displays to reflect the latest research and discoveries in polar science.

Significance

The Fram Museum serves as a tribute to Norway's significant contributions to polar exploration and provides educational opportunities about the scientific and human aspects of these historic expeditions.

Exhibits and Collections

The Fram Ship

Ship Display: The centerpiece of the museum is the Fram, a wooden ship specially designed to withstand the extreme conditions of the polar regions. Visitors can explore the ship's interior, including the crew quarters, dining areas, and scientific laboratories.

Design and Construction: Learn about the Fram's unique design, including its innovative hull construction that allowed it to drift with the polar ice, rather than be crushed by it.

Polar Exploration Exhibits

Fridtjof Nansen: Exhibits highlight Nansen's 1888 Arctic expedition aboard the Fram, including his pioneering drift with the ice and his contributions to polar science and humanitarian work.

Roald Amundsen: Explore Amundsen's 1910-1912 Antarctic expedition, which culminated in the first successful expedition to the South Pole. Exhibits cover his preparations, journey, and achievements.

Scientific Instruments: The museum displays a range of historical scientific instruments used during the expeditions, providing insight into the research conducted in the polar regions.

Interactive Exhibits

Virtual Reality: Engage with virtual reality experiences that simulate polar conditions and provide a closer look at the life and work of polar explorers.

Educational Programs: The museum offers interactive programs and workshops for children and adults, including activities related to polar science and exploration.

Multimedia Presentations

Documentaries and Films: Watch documentaries and films about polar exploration, featuring footage from historic expeditions and interviews with contemporary scientists and explorers.

Location

The Fram Museum is located on the Bygdøy Peninsula in Oslo, an area known for its concentration of museums. The address is: Huk Aveny 32, 0287 Oslo, Norway

Opening and Closing Hours

Regular Hours: The museum is generally open daily from 10:00 AM to 6:00 PM.

Seasonal Variations: Hours may vary during the off-season, and the museum is occasionally closed for special events or maintenance, so it's best to check the official website for current hours.

Visitor Information

Admission Fees

General Admission: There is an entry fee for adults, with discounted rates for seniors, students, and children. Family tickets and annual passes are also available.

Free Days: The museum occasionally offers free admission days or reduced rates for specific groups, such as Oslo residents or students.

Facilities

Café and Restaurant: The museum features a café that offers light meals and refreshments with views of the nearby Oslofjord.

Gift Shop: The gift shop sells a variety of polar-themed merchandise, including books, souvenirs, and educational toys.

Restrooms: Restroom facilities are available within the museum.

Accessibility

Wheelchair Access: The museum is fully accessible to visitors with disabilities, with ramps, elevators, and accessible restrooms.

Guided Tours: Guided tours are available in multiple languages, providing a detailed exploration of the museum's exhibits and the history of polar exploration.

Things to Do

Explore the Fram Ship

Interior Tour: Take your time to explore the Fram's interior, including its living quarters, the galley, and the ship's wheelhouse. Each area is well-preserved and provides a glimpse into the daily life of polar explorers.

Learn About the Expeditions

Interactive Displays: Engage with interactive displays and multimedia presentations to gain a deeper understanding of the challenges and achievements of polar exploration.

Educational Programs: Participate in workshops and educational programs designed to provide hands-on learning about polar science and history.

Watch Films and Documentaries

Film Screenings: Take advantage of the museum's film screenings to see historical footage and documentaries about polar expeditions. These films often provide additional context and personal stories from the explorers.

Visit the Café and Gift Shop

Relax and Refresh: Enjoy a meal or snack at the museum café, which offers a pleasant setting with views of the Oslofjord.

Shop for Souvenirs: Browse the gift shop for unique polar-themed items to remember your visit.

Tips for Visiting

Check for Events: Before your visit, check the museum's website for any special events, temporary exhibits, or educational programs that might be of interest.

Allocate Time: Allow at least two to three hours to fully explore the museum and the Fram ship. Plan extra time if you wish to participate in interactive exhibits or watch films.

Combine Visits: Consider visiting other nearby museums on the Bygdøy Peninsula, such as the Viking Ship Museum or the Norwegian Museum of Cultural History, for a full day of cultural exploration.

Use Public Transport: The museum is accessible by bus and ferry from central Oslo. The Bygdøy Peninsula is served by several bus routes, and a ferry service operates from the city center during the summer months.

Dress Appropriately: The museum is indoors, but be prepared for cooler weather if you plan to explore the surrounding areas of Bygdøy.

Aker Brygge

Aker Brygge is a bustling district located along the waterfront of Oslo, known for its modern buildings, lively atmosphere, and vibrant mix of activities. It's a prime spot for both locals and tourists to enjoy the best of Oslo's urban lifestyle and waterfront charm.

History

Early Development

Industrial Past: Originally, Aker Brygge was a major industrial area, home to shipyards and warehouses. Its history dates back to the 19th century when it was a bustling center for shipbuilding and maritime trade.

Transformation: In the 1980s, the area underwent significant redevelopment. The old industrial buildings were replaced with modern residential and commercial spaces, transforming Aker Brygge into the vibrant waterfront district it is today.

Modern Era

Architectural Revamp: The redevelopment introduced a mix of contemporary architectural styles, with sleek, glass-fronted buildings and stylish waterfront promenades.

Cultural Hub: Aker Brygge has evolved into a cultural and social hub, featuring a variety of restaurants, shops, galleries, and entertainment venues.

Attractions

Waterfront Promenade

Scenic Walks: The waterfront promenade is perfect for leisurely strolls with stunning views of the Oslofjord, the harbor, and the surrounding hills. It's a great spot to enjoy the fresh air and picturesque scenery.

Marina: The marina at Aker Brygge is home to a variety of boats and yachts, adding to the area's nautical charm.

Tjuvholmen

Adjacent District: Tjuvholmen, a neighboring area to Aker Brygge, offers additional attractions, including the Astrup Fearnley Museum of Modern Art, which features contemporary art exhibitions and sculptures.

Beach and Art: Tjuvholmen also has a small beach area and a promenade with public art installations.

Oslo City Hall

Nearby Landmark: Located a short walk from Aker Brygge, Oslo City Hall is an architectural landmark known for its impressive façade and its role as the venue for the Nobel Peace Prize ceremony. Guided tours of the building are available.

Dining and Shopping

Restaurants and Cafés

Varied Cuisine: Aker Brygge boasts a diverse selection of restaurants and cafés, ranging from upscale dining to casual eateries. Options include seafood restaurants, international cuisine, and local Norwegian dishes.

Outdoor Dining: Many restaurants have outdoor seating areas where you can enjoy a meal with a view of the Oslofjord.

Shopping

Retail Options: The area features a range of shops, from high-end boutiques and designer stores to more affordable fashion outlets and specialty shops.

Markets: Seasonal markets and fairs often take place, offering local crafts, artisanal goods, and fresh produce.

Location

Aker Brygge is situated along the Oslo waterfront, easily accessible from central Oslo. The district is located between the City Hall and the Tjuvholmen area.

Opening and Closing Hours

Restaurants and Shops: Opening hours vary by establishment. Generally, shops are open from 10:00 AM to 6:00 PM, with some restaurants and cafés open later into the evening.

Seasonal Variations: Hours may vary during holidays or special events. It's advisable to check individual business hours before planning your visit.

Visitor Information

Transportation

Public Transport: Aker Brygge is easily accessible by public transport. Take the tram to the Aker Brygge stop or use bus services that stop nearby. The area is also well-connected by ferry services from other parts of Oslo.

Walking: The district is pedestrian-friendly, making it easy to explore on foot.

Parking

Parking Facilities: There are parking garages and surface lots available in and around Aker Brygge. Some parking options may be limited during peak times, so consider using public transport if possible.

Accessibility

Wheelchair Access: Aker Brygge is accessible to visitors with disabilities, with ramps, elevators, and well-maintained pathways throughout the area.

Things to Do

Explore the Promenade

Walk and Relax: Take a leisurely walk along the waterfront promenade, enjoy the views, and relax on the benches scattered along the route.

Dine with a View

Enjoy a Meal: Experience Oslo's culinary scene at one of the many waterfront restaurants. Enjoy fresh seafood, Norwegian specialties, and international dishes while taking in the beautiful views.

Visit Tjuvholmen

Art and Beach: Explore the Tjuvholmen district, visit the Astrup Fearnley Museum, and relax at the beach.

Cultural Activities

City Hall Tour: Take a short walk to Oslo City Hall for a guided tour and learn about its architectural significance and history.

Tips for Visiting

Check the Weather: Oslo's weather can be unpredictable, so check the forecast and dress accordingly. Bring layers and a raincoat if needed.

Reserve Ahead: If you plan to dine at popular restaurants, consider making a reservation in advance, especially during peak times.

Explore Nearby Areas: Combine your visit to Aker Brygge with nearby attractions such as the Nobel Peace Center, the Oslo Opera House, or the Akershus Fortress.

Enjoy the Outdoors: If the weather is nice, take advantage of the outdoor seating at cafés and restaurants for a pleasant dining experience.

Plan for Crowds: Aker Brygge can get busy, particularly during summer and weekends. Arrive early to avoid the largest crowds and enjoy a more relaxed experience.

Kon-Tiki Museum

The Kon-Tiki Museum celebrates the Kon-Tiki expedition led by Thor Heyerdahl in 1947. The museum showcases the Kon-Tiki raft, the expedition's equipment, and the cultural significance of the journey. It provides visitors with insights into Heyerdahl's theories about ancient maritime cultures and the adventurous spirit behind his pioneering research.

History of the Kon-Tiki Museum

Origins and Development

Thor Heyerdahl's Expedition: In 1947, Thor Heyerdahl and his crew embarked on a daring voyage across the Pacific Ocean on a raft named Kon-Tiki. The purpose of the expedition was to demonstrate that ancient South American civilizations could have reached Polynesia using similar raft-based technologies.

Museum Establishment: The Kon-Tiki Museum was established in 1950, just a few years after the successful completion of the Kon-Tiki voyage. The museum was created to preserve the raft and to share the story of Heyerdahl's groundbreaking research.

Significance

Exploration and Discovery: The museum is dedicated to Heyerdahl's contributions to the field of anthropology and maritime history. The Kon-Tiki voyage challenged prevailing theories about ancient navigation and cultural exchanges.

Legacy: Heyerdahl's work remains influential in the study of prehistoric oceanic migration and cultural diffusion.

Exhibits and Collections

The Kon-Tiki Raft

Raft Display: The centerpiece of the museum is the original Kon-Tiki raft. Visitors can explore the raft up close and see how it was constructed using traditional materials and techniques.

Construction and Design: Learn about the design and construction of the raft, including its use of balsa wood, ropes, and natural materials.

Expedition Artifacts

Equipment and Supplies: The museum displays the equipment and supplies used during the Kon-Tiki voyage, including navigation tools, provisions, and personal items of the crew.

Photographs and Documents: Explore a collection of photographs, journals, and documents that chronicle the expedition and provide insight into the crew's experiences.

Interactive Exhibits

Voyage Simulation: Engage with interactive exhibits that simulate aspects of the Kon-Tiki voyage, including navigation and survival challenges faced by the crew.

Educational Programs: The museum offers educational programs and workshops for visitors of all ages, focusing on maritime history and exploration.

Thor Heyerdahl's Other Expeditions

Ra Expeditions: The museum also covers Heyerdahl's other significant expeditions, such as the Ra expeditions, which aimed to prove that ancient Egyptians could have traveled across the Atlantic to the Americas.

Cultural Exhibits: Explore artifacts and displays related to Heyerdahl's studies of ancient civilizations and their potential maritime connections.

Location

The Kon-Tiki Museum is located on the Bygdøy Peninsula in Oslo, a picturesque area known for its concentration of museums. The address is: Bygdøy Allé 36, 0286 Oslo, Norway

Opening and Closing Hours

Regular Hours: The museum is generally open daily from 10:00 AM to 5:00 PM.

Seasonal Variations: Hours may vary during the off-season or holidays. It's advisable to check the official website for current hours and any special closures.

Visitor Information

Admission Fees

General Admission: There is an entry fee for adults, with reduced rates for seniors, students, and children. Family tickets and group rates are also available.

Free Days: The museum occasionally offers free admission days or discounted rates for specific groups, such as Oslo residents or students.

Facilities

Café and Restaurant: The museum features a café that offers refreshments and light meals. Enjoy a snack while overlooking the surrounding natural beauty.

Gift Shop: The gift shop sells a range of souvenirs, including books on Thor Heyerdahl's expeditions, replica artifacts, and other related merchandise.

Restrooms: Restroom facilities are available within the museum.

Accessibility

Wheelchair Access: The museum is accessible to visitors with disabilities, with ramps, elevators, and accessible restrooms.

Guided Tours: Guided tours are available in multiple languages, providing detailed explanations of the exhibits and Heyerdahl's expeditions.

Things to Do

Explore the Kon-Tiki Raft

Detailed Inspection: Take your time to explore the Kon-Tiki raft and learn about its construction, design, and the challenges faced during the voyage.

Learn About the Expedition

Interactive Displays: Engage with interactive exhibits to gain a deeper understanding of the voyage, including the navigation techniques and survival strategies used by Heyerdahl and his crew.

Visit the Café

Relax and Refresh: Enjoy a meal or snack at the museum café, which offers a pleasant setting to relax and reflect on the exhibits.

Shop for Souvenirs

Unique Items: Browse the gift shop for unique souvenirs related to Thor Heyerdahl's expeditions, including books, replica artifacts, and educational materials.

Tips for Visiting

Check for Special Events: Before your visit, check the museum's website for any special events, temporary exhibits, or educational programs that might be of interest.

Allocate Time: Plan to spend at least 1-2 hours exploring the museum and the Kon-Tiki raft. Allow extra time if you wish to participate in interactive exhibits or guided tours.

Combine Visits: Consider visiting other nearby museums on the Bygdøy Peninsula, such as the Viking Ship Museum or the Norwegian Museum of Cultural History, for a full day of cultural exploration.

Use Public Transport: The museum is accessible by bus from central Oslo. The Bygdøy Peninsula is served by several bus routes, and a ferry service operates from the city center during the summer months.

Dress Appropriately: The museum is indoors, but be prepared for cooler weather if you plan to explore the surrounding areas of Bygdøy.

Royal Palace

The Royal Palace is the official residence of the Norwegian monarch, currently King Harald V. Located in the heart of Oslo, the palace serves as the venue for official state functions, ceremonies, and royal events. It is an iconic representation of Norway's royal heritage and a focal point of national pride.

History

Origins and Construction

Initial Plans: The idea of constructing a new royal residence for Norway's monarchs emerged in the early 19th century, following Norway's independence from Denmark in 1814.

Architectural Design: The palace was designed by the Danish architect Hans Linstow in a neoclassical style. Construction began in 1824, and the building was completed in 1848.

Royal Residence: The palace became the official residence of King Oscar I and has been the royal residence of Norwegian monarchs ever since.

Historical Significance

Political and Cultural Role: The Royal Palace has played a central role in Norway's political and cultural life, hosting state functions, official ceremonies, and significant royal events.

Modern Era: In contemporary times, the palace continues to serve as the residence of the Norwegian royal family and the center of ceremonial activities.

Architectural Features

Exterior Design

Neoclassical Style: The Royal Palace is designed in a neoclassical architectural style, characterized by its clean lines, symmetrical façade, and classical columns.

Grand Facade: The palace features a grand façade with a central portico supported by Doric columns, adding to its imposing and elegant appearance.

Interior Design

State Rooms: The palace boasts a range of opulent state rooms, including the Hall of Mirrors, the Ballroom, and the Throne Room. These rooms are decorated with luxurious furnishings, ornate chandeliers, and exquisite artworks.

Private Apartments: The royal family's private apartments are not open to the public but are located within the palace, providing a glimpse into the royal lifestyle.

Gardens and Grounds

Palace Park: The palace is surrounded by a beautifully landscaped park, known as the Palace Park (Slottsparken). The park features manicured lawns, walking paths, and decorative fountains.

Changing of the Guard: The park is also the site of the daily Changing of the Guard ceremony, which attracts many visitors.

Visitor Information

Opening Hours and Tours

Guided Tours: The Royal Palace offers guided tours during the summer months, typically from late June to mid-August. Tours provide insight into the history, architecture, and royal life associated with the palace.

Winter Visits: During the winter, the palace is not open for tours, but the exterior and the surrounding park can be visited.

Admission Fees

Tour Fees: There is an admission fee for guided tours of the Royal Palace. Prices vary depending on age, with discounts available for children, students, and seniors.

Free Visits: The exterior of the palace and the Changing of the Guard ceremony are free to view.

Facilities

Gift Shop: The Royal Palace has a gift shop where visitors can purchase souvenirs related to the palace and Norwegian royalty.

Restrooms: Restroom facilities are available within the palace grounds.

Accessibility

Wheelchair Access: The palace is wheelchair accessible, with ramps and elevators available for visitors with disabilities.

Guided Tours: Some tours are specifically designed to accommodate visitors with special needs. It is advisable to contact the palace in advance to make arrangements.

Things to Do

Explore the Palace Interior

Guided Tour: Join a guided tour to explore the state rooms, learn about the palace's history, and gain insight into royal life and ceremonies.

Architectural Highlights: Take note of the neoclassical design elements, including the elegant columns, grand staircases, and opulent decorations.

Enjoy the Palace Park

Stroll in the Park: Take a leisurely walk in the Palace Park, enjoy the green spaces, and admire the decorative fountains and sculptures.

Watch the Changing of the Guard: Witness the daily Changing of the Guard ceremony, which takes place at 1:30 PM, and observe the ceremonial precision of the Norwegian Royal Guard.

Visit Nearby Attractions

National Theatre: Located near the Royal Palace, the National Theatre offers a range of performances and is worth a visit if you enjoy the arts.

Karl Johans Gate: Explore the main street of Oslo, which runs from the Royal Palace to the Central Station, and enjoy shopping, dining, and cultural attractions along the way.

Tips for Visiting

Book in Advance: If you plan to take a guided tour, book tickets in advance, especially during the peak tourist season.

Check Tour Dates: Verify the tour dates and availability before your visit, as tours are limited to specific months.

Arrive Early: Arrive early to explore the surrounding park, find a good viewing spot for the Changing of the Guard, and enjoy the tranquil atmosphere before the tours start.

Dress Appropriately: Wear comfortable shoes for walking and dress in layers, as the weather in Oslo can be unpredictable.

Respect the Rules: Follow the palace's rules and guidelines during your visit, including photography restrictions and behavior expectations.

Oslo Cathedral (Oslo Domkirke)

Oslo Cathedral is the main church of the Church of Norway's Oslo Diocese and serves as a prominent religious site in Oslo. Its central location, historical significance, and beautiful interior make it a notable destination for both visitors and locals.

History

Early Beginnings

Construction: The original cathedral was built in 1697 on the site of a previous church that was destroyed in a fire. The current building, designed by architect Daniel von der Linne, was completed in 1697 and inaugurated in 1699.

Architectural Style: The cathedral was constructed in a Baroque style, characterized by its ornate detailing and elegant design.

Significant Events

Royal Events: Oslo Cathedral has hosted numerous significant events, including royal weddings, state ceremonies, and important religious services. Notably, it was the venue for the wedding of King Harald V and Queen Sonja in 1968.

Renovations: Over the years, the cathedral has undergone several renovations to preserve its historical features and adapt to modern needs. Notable restoration projects include the renovation of the interior and the replacement of the original roof.

Modern Era

Cultural Role: Today, Oslo Cathedral remains an active place of worship and a popular tourist attraction. It plays a central role in the city's religious and cultural life, hosting various events, concerts, and services.

Architectural Features

Exterior Design

Baroque Style: The cathedral is built in the Baroque architectural style, characterized by its grand façade, decorative details, and harmonious proportions.

Clock Tower: One of the most prominent features of Oslo Cathedral is its clock tower, which stands out against the Oslo skyline and serves as a local landmark.

Interior Design

Altarpiece: The cathedral's interior features a stunning altarpiece, which was created by artist Emanuel Vigeland in 1904. The altarpiece depicts the Last Supper and is a central focal point of the cathedral's design.

Woodwork and Paintings: The interior is adorned with intricate woodwork, elegant chandeliers, and beautiful paintings. Notable elements include the vaulted ceilings, decorative organ pipes, and richly decorated pews.

Stained Glass Windows: The cathedral's stained glass windows add a colorful and serene atmosphere to the interior, enhancing the overall aesthetic experience.

Organ

Historic Organ: Oslo Cathedral houses a historic pipe organ, which is a key feature of the church's musical heritage. The organ is used for various services, concerts, and events throughout the year.

Visitor Information

Opening Hours

Regular Hours: Oslo Cathedral is generally open to visitors during weekdays and weekends. The opening hours may vary, so it's advisable to check the cathedral's official website or contact them directly for the most up-to-date information.

Services and Events: During services and special events, the cathedral may be closed to tourists. Visitors should check the schedule to plan their visit accordingly.

Admission Fees

Entry: Entry to Oslo Cathedral is usually free, although donations are welcomed to support the maintenance and preservation of the building.

Special Tours: Guided tours of the cathedral may be available for a fee, providing deeper insights into the history, architecture, and significance of the building.

Facilities

Gift Shop: The cathedral features a small gift shop where visitors can purchase religious items, souvenirs, and books related to the cathedral and its history.

Restrooms: Restroom facilities are available within the cathedral or nearby.

Accessibility

Wheelchair Access: The cathedral is accessible to visitors with disabilities, with ramps and accessible restrooms available. However, due to the historic nature of the building, some areas may have limited accessibility.

Guided Tours: Some tours are designed to accommodate visitors with special needs. Contact the cathedral in advance to arrange accessible tours if required.

Things to Do

Explore the Interior

Admire the Altarpiece: Take time to appreciate the detailed altarpiece and the intricate artwork that adorns the cathedral.

View the Organ: If possible, attend an organ concert or service to hear the historic pipe organ in action.

Attend a Service or Concert

Participate in Services: Attend a regular church service to experience the cathedral's role in the local community.

Enjoy a Concert: Oslo Cathedral hosts various musical events and concerts throughout the year. Check the schedule to see if there are any performances during your visit.

Stroll Around the Cathedral

Exterior Views: Explore the exterior of the cathedral, including the clock tower and the surrounding area. The cathedral's location offers picturesque views and a chance to experience the local architecture.

Tips for Visiting

Check the Schedule: Before visiting, check the cathedral's schedule for services, events, and tours to avoid any disruptions during your visit.

Respect the Space: As an active place of worship, be respectful of the cathedral's religious and cultural significance. Follow any guidelines provided by the staff.

Dress Modestly: While casual attire is generally acceptable, it's advisable to dress modestly and respectfully when visiting religious sites.

Plan for Crowds: The cathedral may be busier during weekends, holidays, or special events. Consider visiting during quieter times for a more peaceful experience.

Combine Visits: If you have time, explore nearby attractions such as the Oslo City Hall or the National Gallery, which are located within walking distance.

The Ultimate Oslo Travel Guide (2025 Edition)

Chapter 6: Neighborhood of Oslo

City Center (Sentrum)

Sentrum is Oslo's central business district and cultural hub, characterized by its lively atmosphere, iconic landmarks, and diverse range of activities. It's the focal point of Oslo's urban life, with a blend of historical sites, modern amenities, and beautiful architecture.

Historical and Cultural Landmarks

Oslo City Hall (Rådhuset)

Overview: A striking building known for its distinctive red-brick architecture and its role as the venue for the Nobel Peace Prize ceremony.

Highlights: Grand halls, murals depicting Norwegian history, and guided tours available.

Akershus Fortress (Akershus Festning)

Overview: A medieval castle and fortress with panoramic views of Oslofjord, rich in history and architecture.

Highlights: The fortress grounds, historical exhibits, and guided tours.

Oslo Cathedral (Oslo Domkirke)

Overview: The city's main church, featuring Baroque architecture and a significant role in local religious and ceremonial life.

Highlights: The altarpiece, organ concerts, and historical interiors.

National Gallery (Nasjonalgalleriet)

Overview: Home to Norway's largest collection of artworks, including Edvard Munch's "The Scream."

Highlights: Norwegian and international art collections, including masterpieces by Munch and other renowned artists.

Stortinget (Parliament Building)

Overview: The seat of Norway's national parliament, notable for its architectural style and political significance.

Highlights: The building's exterior, guided tours available by appointment.

Shopping and Dining

Karl Johans Gate

Overview: Oslo's main shopping street, lined with a mix of international brands, local boutiques, cafes, and restaurants.

Highlights: Shopping opportunities, street performers, and vibrant atmosphere.

Aker Brygge

Overview: A modern waterfront area known for its trendy shops, restaurants, and lively promenade.

Highlights: Dining with views of the fjord, outdoor seating areas, and seasonal markets.

Grünerløkka

Overview: A trendy district adjacent to Sentrum, known for its hip boutiques, cafes, and street art.

Highlights: Independent shops, vintage stores, and lively bars.

Cultural Venues

Oslo Opera House (Operahuset)

Overview: A modern architectural marvel offering world-class opera and ballet performances.

Highlights: The building's sloping roof with panoramic views, guided tours, and performances.

The Norwegian Museum of Cultural History (Norsk Folkemuseum)

Overview: An open-air museum showcasing Norwegian cultural history and traditional architecture.

Highlights: Historic buildings, folk art, and seasonal events.

History of Sentrum

Early Development

Origins: The area around Sentrum has been central to Oslo's development since the city was founded in the 11th century. It was initially a trading hub and later evolved into a commercial and administrative center.

Medieval Oslo: Early landmarks like the Akershus Fortress date back to medieval times, reflecting Oslo's historical importance.

Modern Era

19th Century Growth: In the 19th century, Sentrum saw significant urban development, with the construction of key buildings like the City Hall and Stortinget.

Post-War Development: After World War II, Oslo's City Center underwent modernization and expansion, incorporating new architectural styles and urban planning concepts.

Getting Around Sentrum

Public Transportation

Metro (T-Bane): Sentrum is well-served by Oslo's metro system, with several lines passing through the area. Key stations include Jernbanetorget and Nationaltheatret.

Trams and Buses: Numerous tram and bus routes connect Sentrum with other parts of Oslo and surrounding neighborhoods.

Walking

Walkable Area: Sentrum is compact and pedestrian-friendly, with many attractions, shops, and dining options within walking distance of each other.

Cycling

Bike-Friendly: Oslo has a network of cycling paths, and renting a bike is a convenient way to explore Sentrum and nearby areas.

Visitor Information

Opening Hours

Attractions: Opening hours vary by attraction. Many museums and landmarks are open from late June to mid-August for extended hours. Check individual sites for the latest information.

Admission Fees

Varies by Site: Fees vary for museums and attractions. Some sites, like city parks and historic buildings, may offer free admission or have nominal fees.

Facilities

Dining: Sentrum offers a wide range of dining options, from casual cafes to fine dining restaurants. The Aker Brygge area is particularly known for its diverse culinary scene.

Restrooms: Public restrooms are available in shopping centers, larger public buildings, and some outdoor areas.

Accessibility

Wheelchair Access: Most major attractions and public transportation options are wheelchair accessible. Check individual sites for specific accessibility features.

Tips for Visiting

Start at City Hall: Begin your exploration at Oslo City Hall to get a sense of the city's history and architecture.

Explore Karl Johans Gate: Stroll down this main shopping street to experience Oslo's vibrant city life and do some shopping.

Visit Museums: Allocate time to visit key museums like the National Gallery and Oslo Cathedral to experience Oslo's cultural heritage.

Enjoy Outdoor Spaces: Spend time at Aker Brygge and other waterfront areas to enjoy views of Oslofjord and relax in outdoor cafes.

Check Event Schedules: Look up event schedules for performances at the Oslo Opera House and other cultural venues to enhance your visit.

Grünerløkka

Grünerløkka is often compared to other hipster neighborhoods around the world, with its mix of vintage shops, street art, and bustling cafes. It's a favorite among locals and tourists alike for its relaxed atmosphere and cultural richness. The area is characterized by its bohemian vibe, historical architecture, and a strong sense of community.

Historic and Cultural Sites

Mathallen Oslo

Overview: A food hall featuring a wide range of gourmet food stalls, local produce, and international cuisine.

Highlights: Diverse food offerings, local specialties, and a lively market atmosphere.

Grünerløkka Brewery

Overview: A local brewery known for its craft beers and vibrant beer garden.

Highlights: Beer tastings, brewery tours, and a casual atmosphere.

Løkka's Street Art

Overview: Grünerløkka is renowned for its colorful street art and murals.

Highlights: Walking tours to discover various street art pieces and murals scattered throughout the neighborhood.

Parks and Outdoor Spaces

Birkelunden Park

Overview: A popular park in Grünerløkka with green spaces, playgrounds, and a lively atmosphere.

Highlights: Farmers' markets, picnicking areas, and local events.

St. Hanshaugen Park

Overview: A large park located just west of Grünerløkka, offering panoramic views of Oslo and recreational facilities.

Highlights: Walking trails, viewpoints, and open spaces for outdoor activities.

Shopping and Dining

Vintage Shops and Boutiques

Overview: Grünerløkka is known for its array of vintage shops, independent boutiques, and artisan stores.

Highlights: Unique fashion finds, retro furniture, and handmade crafts.

Cafés and Restaurants

Overview: The neighborhood boasts a variety of cozy cafes and trendy restaurants offering both Norwegian and international cuisine.

Highlights: Hip cafes, brunch spots, and dining options with a focus on locally sourced ingredients.

Art and Culture

Kunstnernes Hus

Overview: An art gallery and cultural venue showcasing contemporary art and hosting various exhibitions and events.

Highlights: Art exhibitions, cultural events, and workshops.

Grünerløkka Museum

Overview: A small museum dedicated to the history and development of the Grünerløkka area.

Highlights: Exhibits on local history, development, and the cultural evolution of the neighborhood.

History of Grünerløkka

Early Development

Origins: Grünerløkka was originally a residential area established in the late 19th century. It developed as a working-class neighborhood with a mix of industrial and residential buildings.

Industrial Era: During the industrial era, Grünerløkka became known for its factories and working-class communities. The area's industrial heritage is still reflected in some of its architecture and layout.

Transformation

Cultural Shift: In the latter half of the 20th century, Grünerløkka underwent significant gentrification and cultural transformation. The neighborhood shifted from an industrial and working-class area to a vibrant cultural hub.

Artistic Hub: Today, Grünerløkka is celebrated for its artistic and bohemian atmosphere, with a focus on creative industries, independent businesses, and cultural events.

Getting Around Grünerløkka

Public Transportation

Trams: Several tram lines serve Grünerløkka, including lines 11, 12, and 13, making it easy to travel to and from the city center.

Buses: Multiple bus routes connect Grünerløkka with other parts of Oslo, including routes 21, 37, and 54.

Walking and Cycling

Walkable Area: Grünerløkka is a pedestrian-friendly neighborhood with many attractions and amenities within walking distance of each other.

Cycling: Oslo has a network of cycling paths, and renting a bike is a convenient way to explore Grünerløkka and its surroundings.

Visitor Information

Opening Hours

Shops and Cafés: Hours vary by establishment, with many shops and cafes open daily from morning to evening. Some businesses may have extended hours on weekends.

Museums and Galleries: Opening hours for museums and galleries vary, with many open from late spring to early autumn for extended hours. Check individual sites for specific times and dates.

Admission Fees

Museums and Galleries: Admission fees for museums and galleries may vary, with some offering free entry or discounted rates for students, seniors, and families.

Public Spaces: Parks and outdoor spaces are generally free to access.

Facilities

Dining: Grünerløkka offers a wide range of dining options, from casual cafes to upscale restaurants. Many establishments focus on locally sourced ingredients and innovative cuisine.

Restrooms: Public restrooms are available in parks, larger public buildings, and some cafes or restaurants.

Accessibility

Wheelchair Access: Most major attractions, shops, and public transportation options in Grünerløkka are wheelchair accessible. Check individual sites for specific accessibility features.

Tips for Visiting

Explore on Foot: Take your time walking through Grünerløkka to fully appreciate its street art, unique shops, and lively atmosphere.

Visit Local Markets: If your visit coincides with a farmers' market or local event, be sure to check it out for local produce and crafts.

Enjoy a Café Culture: Spend time in one of Grünerløkka's many cozy cafes to experience the local coffee culture and relaxed vibe.

Discover Street Art: Consider joining a street art tour to learn more about the neighborhood's vibrant mural and graffiti scene.

Check for Events: Look up local events, exhibitions, and performances happening during your visit to make the most of Grünerløkka's cultural offerings.

Aker Brygge and Tjuvholmen

Aker Brygge and Tjuvholmen are adjacent neighborhoods known for their waterfront promenades, modern buildings, and bustling atmosphere. Both areas have been developed from former industrial and docklands into thriving cultural and recreational hubs.

Key Attractions and Points of Interest

Aker Brygge

Waterfront Promenade

Overview: A popular pedestrian area lined with restaurants, cafes, and shops, offering stunning views of Oslofjord and the surrounding landscape.

Highlights: Scenic walks, outdoor seating, and views of ferries and boats.

Aker Brygge Shopping Center

Overview: A shopping complex featuring a variety of international and local brands, along with dining options.

Highlights: Fashion stores, specialty shops, and gourmet food.

Nobel Peace Center

Overview: A museum dedicated to the Nobel Peace Prize, showcasing the history and impact of the award.

Highlights: Exhibits on Nobel laureates, interactive displays, and multimedia presentations.

Oslo Maritime Museum

Overview: Located at the end of Aker Brygge, this museum focuses on Norway's maritime heritage and history.

Highlights: Ship models, maritime artifacts, and interactive exhibits.

Tjuvholmen

Astrup Fearnley Museum of Modern Art

Overview: A prominent contemporary art museum with a striking architectural design by Renzo Piano.

Highlights: Rotating exhibitions of modern and contemporary art, including works by international and Norwegian artists.

Tjuvholmen Sculpture Park

Overview: An outdoor park featuring a collection of sculptures by various artists, integrated into the urban landscape.

Highlights: Sculptures set against the backdrop of Oslofjord, providing an open-air art experience.

The Thief Hotel

Overview: A luxury hotel known for its design, comfort, and location on the waterfront.

Highlights: Stylish rooms, a renowned restaurant, and views of the fjord.

Tjuvholmen Beach

Overview: A small, man-made beach area perfect for relaxing and enjoying the waterfront during warmer months.

Highlights: Sunbathing, swimming, and enjoying the seaside atmosphere.

History of Aker Brygge and Tjuvholmen

Aker Brygge

Industrial Past: Aker Brygge was once a bustling industrial area and shipyard. The transformation began in the late 1980s and early 1990s when the area was redeveloped into a modern waterfront district.

Revitalization: The redevelopment aimed to preserve the historical character while integrating new residential, commercial, and recreational spaces.

Tjuvholmen

Historical Development: Tjuvholmen has a history as a dock and industrial area. It was transformed in the early 2000s as part of Oslo's waterfront redevelopment project.

Modernization: The area was designed to create a cultural and residential hub, featuring modern architecture and public art.

Getting Around Aker Brygge and Tjuvholmen

Public Transportation

Trams: The area is well-connected by tram lines, including lines 12 and 13, with stops at Aker Brygge.

Buses: Several bus routes serve the area, providing easy access to other parts of Oslo.

Walking and Cycling

Pedestrian-Friendly: Both Aker Brygge and Tjuvholmen are pedestrian-friendly, with wide promenades and easy access to various attractions.

Cycling: Oslo has an extensive network of cycling paths, and renting a bike is a great way to explore these waterfront areas.

Visitor Information

Opening Hours

Shops and Cafés: Most shops and dining establishments in Aker Brygge and Tjuvholmen are open daily, with extended hours during the tourist season.

Museums and Galleries: Opening hours vary by institution. The Nobel Peace Center and Astrup Fearnley Museum generally open from morning to early evening, with specific hours available on their websites.

Admission Fees

Museums: Fees for the Nobel Peace Center and Astrup Fearnley Museum vary, with discounts available for students, seniors, and children.

Public Spaces: The waterfront promenade and public parks are free to access.

Facilities

Dining: Aker Brygge and Tjuvholmen offer a range of dining options, from casual cafes to fine dining restaurants, many with outdoor seating and fjord views.

Restrooms: Public restrooms are available in shopping centers, larger public buildings, and some restaurants.

Accessibility

Wheelchair Access: Both Aker Brygge and Tjuvholmen are designed to be accessible, with wheelchair-friendly paths and facilities. Check individual sites for specific accessibility features.

Tips for Visiting

Enjoy the Waterfront: Take advantage of the scenic views by strolling along the promenade and relaxing by the fjord.

Explore Museums: Allocate time to visit the Nobel Peace Center and Astrup Fearnley Museum to experience Oslo's cultural and artistic offerings.

Check for Events: Look for local events, outdoor concerts, or seasonal markets happening in the area to enhance your visit.

Relax at the Beach: If visiting during warmer months, spend some time at Tjuvholmen Beach to enjoy the sun and water.

Try Local Cuisine: Sample local seafood and Norwegian dishes at the various dining options available along the waterfront.

Majorstuen

Majorstuen is a popular and bustling neighborhood that acts as a key commercial and residential hub. It is well-known for its bustling shopping streets, diverse dining options, and convenient access to public transportation. The area also features several historical landmarks and cultural attractions, making it an appealing destination for both tourists and locals.

Key Attractions and Points of Interest

Shopping and Dining

Bogstadveien

Overview: One of Oslo's main shopping streets, known for its wide range of shops, boutiques, and eateries.

Highlights: International brands, local fashion stores, and a variety of cafes and restaurants offering both Norwegian and international cuisine.

Majorstuen Shopping Center

Overview: A local shopping mall featuring a mix of retail stores, eateries, and essential services.

Highlights: Shops for clothing, electronics, and groceries, as well as dining options within the mall.

Vigeland Museum Café

Overview: Located near the Vigeland Park, this café offers a cozy setting and a menu featuring local dishes.

Highlights: Light meals, pastries, and coffee, with views of the surrounding park.

Cultural and Historical Sites

Vigeland Park (Frogner Park)

Overview: One of Oslo's most famous parks, featuring over 200 sculptures by Gustav Vigeland.

Highlights: Iconic sculptures, beautifully landscaped gardens, and the Vigeland Museum located within the park.

The Norwegian Museum of Cultural History (Norsk Folkemuseum)

Overview: An open-air museum showcasing traditional Norwegian life with historic buildings and folk art.

Highlights: Historic buildings, cultural exhibits, and traditional Norwegian crafts.

Majorstuen Church

Overview: A historic church known for its beautiful architecture and serene atmosphere.

Highlights: Gothic Revival architecture, historical artifacts, and peaceful surroundings.

Recreational Areas

Vigeland Park Playground

Overview: A large playground located within Vigeland Park, ideal for families with children.

Highlights: Play equipment, open spaces, and proximity to the park's attractions.

St. Hanshaugen Park

Overview: A nearby park offering expansive green spaces, walking paths, and panoramic views of Oslo.

Highlights: Hiking trails, viewpoints, and recreational areas.

History of Majorstuen

Early Development

Origins: Majorstuen was initially developed in the late 19th and early 20th centuries as a residential area, with a focus on expanding Oslo's housing and infrastructure.

Urban Growth: The area saw significant growth and development, becoming a key commercial and residential district due to its strategic location and access to transportation.

Modern Era

Commercial Expansion: In the latter half of the 20th century, Majorstuen evolved into a bustling commercial hub, with the development of shopping streets, dining options, and cultural institutions.

Community and Culture: Today, Majorstuen maintains its status as a vibrant neighborhood with a strong community feel, diverse amenities, and cultural attractions.

Getting Around Majorstuen

Public Transportation

Metro (T-Bane): Majorstuen is well-connected by the Oslo Metro, with several lines serving the area. The Majorstuen Station is a key transit point.

Trams and Buses: Various tram and bus lines provide easy access to other parts of Oslo, including routes 12 and 13 for trams, and multiple bus routes.

Walking and Cycling

Pedestrian-Friendly: Majorstuen is a walkable area with many attractions, shops, and restaurants within easy reach.

Cycling: Oslo's cycling paths make it convenient to explore Majorstuen and the surrounding areas by bike. Bike rentals are available in the city.

Visitor Information

Opening Hours

Shops and Cafés: Most shops and dining establishments in Majorstuen are open daily, with extended hours during weekends and peak tourist seasons.

Cultural Sites: Museums and historical sites have varied opening hours. Check specific sites for the latest information.

Admission Fees

Museums: Fees for museums like the Vigeland Museum and the Norwegian Museum of Cultural History may vary, with discounts available for students, seniors, and children.

Public Spaces: Parks and public recreational areas are generally free to access.

Facilities

Dining: Majorstuen offers a range of dining options, from casual cafes to fine dining restaurants, many with outdoor seating.

Restrooms: Public restrooms are available in shopping centers, larger public buildings, and some cafes or restaurants.

Accessibility

Wheelchair Access: Majorstuen is designed to be accessible, with wheelchair-friendly paths and facilities. Check individual sites for specific accessibility features.

Tips for Visiting

Explore Bogstadveien: Spend time strolling along Bogstadveien to enjoy shopping and dining in one of Oslo's key commercial streets.

Visit Vigeland Park: Allocate time to explore Vigeland Park and its impressive collection of sculptures and beautiful gardens.

Check Out Majorstuen Church: If interested in historical architecture, visit Majorstuen Church for its Gothic Revival style and tranquil atmosphere.

Relax in Parks: Spend some time in nearby parks like Vigeland Park and St. Hanshaugen for a relaxing break and outdoor enjoyment.

Use Public Transit: Take advantage of Majorstuen's excellent public transportation options to explore other parts of Oslo conveniently.

Frogner

Frogner is distinguished by its beautiful residential streets, historic buildings, and proximity to some of Oslo's most famous cultural sites. The neighborhood is known for its upscale atmosphere, cultural landmarks, and vibrant local life. Visitors can explore stunning parks, historic sites, and a variety of dining and shopping options, all within a scenic and serene environment.

Key Attractions and Points of Interest

Parks and Green Spaces

Vigeland Park (Frogner Park)

Overview: Oslo's largest park, featuring over 200 sculptures by Gustav Vigeland. It's a central attraction in Frogner and a must-visit for anyone interested in art and outdoor beauty.

Highlights: Iconic sculptures, beautifully landscaped gardens, and the Vigeland Museum.

Frognerparken

Overview: A spacious and scenic park adjacent to Vigeland Park, ideal for leisurely walks and picnics.

Highlights: Open green spaces, walking paths, and playgrounds.

Cultural and Historical Sites

Frogner Church

Overview: A historic church with Gothic Revival architecture, serving as a local place of worship and a historical landmark.

Highlights: Architectural details, historical significance, and a serene setting.

Oslo City Museum

Overview: Located in Frogner, this museum offers insights into Oslo's history and urban development.

Highlights: Exhibits on Oslo's past, historical artifacts, and interactive displays.

The Royal Palace

Overview: Although technically just outside Frogner, the Royal Palace is a major landmark close to the neighborhood. It serves as the official residence of the Norwegian monarch.

Highlights: Guided tours of the palace, the changing of the guard, and beautiful surrounding gardens.

Shopping and Dining

Frognerveien

Overview: A major street in Frogner with a variety of shops, boutiques, and cafes.

Highlights: Local boutiques, specialty stores, and charming cafes.

Majorstuen Shopping Center

Overview: Located nearby, this shopping center offers a range of retail stores, dining options, and essential services.

Highlights: Fashion stores, grocery shops, and dining facilities.

Architectural Highlights

Historic Residences

Overview: Frogner is known for its elegant and historic residential buildings, showcasing classic Norwegian architecture.

Highlights: Stately homes, charming apartment buildings, and tree-lined streets.

Frogner Manor

Overview: A historical building with beautiful architecture, often used for cultural events and private functions.

Highlights: Architectural beauty and historical significance.

History of Frogner

Early Development

Origins: Frogner was developed in the late 19th and early 20th centuries as a prestigious residential area, attracting affluent families and professionals.

Urban Growth: The neighborhood evolved from agricultural land to a bustling urban area, characterized by its elegant architecture and green spaces.

Cultural Significance

Cultural Hub: Over the years, Frogner has become known for its cultural institutions, historic buildings, and vibrant community life. The development of Vigeland Park and the proximity to the Royal Palace further enhanced its cultural significance.

Getting Around Frogner

Public Transportation

Trams and Buses: Frogner is well-served by tram and bus lines, providing easy access to other parts of Oslo. Tram lines 12 and 13 and several bus routes connect the neighborhood to the city center and beyond.

Metro (T-Bane): The nearby Majorstuen Metro Station offers convenient access to the Oslo Metro system.

Walking and Cycling

Pedestrian-Friendly: Frogner is a walkable area with many attractions and amenities within easy reach. The scenic streets and parks make it ideal for leisurely walks.

Cycling: Oslo's network of cycling paths extends into Frogner, making it convenient to explore by bike.

The Ultimate Oslo Travel Guide (2025 Edition)

Visitor Information

Opening Hours

Shops and Cafés: Most shops and dining establishments in Frogner are open daily, with extended hours during weekends and peak tourist seasons.

Cultural Sites: Museums and historical sites have varied opening hours. Check specific sites for the latest information.

Admission Fees

Museums: Fees for museums like the Oslo City Museum may vary, with discounts available for students, seniors, and children.

Public Spaces: Parks and public recreational areas are generally free to access.

Facilities

Dining: Frogner offers a range of dining options, from cozy cafes to upscale restaurants, many with outdoor seating and views of the surrounding streets and parks.

Restrooms: Public restrooms are available in shopping centers, larger public buildings, and some cafes or restaurants.

Accessibility

Wheelchair Access: Frogner is designed to be accessible, with wheelchair-friendly paths and facilities. Check individual sites for specific accessibility features.

Tips for Visiting

Explore Vigeland Park: Allocate time to fully explore Vigeland Park and its impressive collection of sculptures and gardens.

Visit the Oslo City Museum: Learn about Oslo's history and development by visiting the Oslo City Museum in Frogner.

Enjoy Local Dining: Take advantage of Frogner's dining options, from charming cafes to elegant restaurants.

Stroll Through Historic Streets: Spend time walking through Frogner's tree-lined streets and admire its elegant architecture and historic residences.

Check Out Nearby Attractions: Don't miss the nearby Royal Palace and Majorstuen Shopping Center for a full Oslo experience.

Chapter 7: Accommodation Options in Oslo

Luxury Hotels

For tourists seeking a lavish stay in Oslo, the city offers an array of luxury hotels that blend elegance with top-notch amenities. These hotels provide impeccable service, opulent rooms, and prime locations, ensuring a memorable and comfortable experience. From stunning fjord views to gourmet dining and exclusive spa services, Oslo's luxury accommodations cater to travelers who desire the finest in comfort and style. Explore the city in ultimate sophistication with a stay at one of Oslo's premier luxury hotels.

Top 5 Luxury Hotels

1. **The Thief**

The Thief is a luxury boutique hotel located in the heart of Oslo's vibrant Tjuvholmen district. Known for its sleek, modern design and artistic flair, it caters to both leisure and business travelers with its elegant accommodations and top-notch services.

Location

Address: Landgangen 1, 0252 Oslo, Norway

Proximity: The Thief is situated on the Tjuvholmen peninsula, adjacent to the Oslofjord and within walking distance of several key attractions:

Aker Brygge: 5 minutes by foot

Oslo City Center (Karl Johans Gate): 15-20 minutes by foot

Astrup Fearnley Museum of Modern Art: 5 minutes by foot

Oslo Opera House: 10 minutes by taxi or public transport

Highlights

Design: The hotel features a contemporary design with a focus on art and luxury. Its interiors are a blend of Scandinavian minimalism and high-end opulence, including curated art pieces throughout the property.

Views: Many rooms offer stunning views of the Oslofjord and the cityscape.

Spa and Wellness

Spa: The Thief's spa, known as **The Thief Spa**, offers a range of treatments designed to relax and rejuvenate. Facilities include a sauna, steam room, and a variety of massages and beauty treatments.

Fitness: The hotel also features a well-equipped gym with modern fitness equipment, ensuring guests can maintain their workout routine.

Bars

The Thief Bar: Located on the rooftop, this bar offers a sophisticated setting with panoramic views of Oslo. It's an ideal spot for enjoying cocktails or a glass of wine while taking in the city skyline.

The Lounge: A stylish space in the hotel lobby where guests can relax with a drink, enjoy light snacks, or socialize in a chic environment.

Events and Conferences

Meeting Facilities: The Thief offers well-appointed meeting rooms and conference facilities. These spaces are equipped with state-of-the-art technology and can be customized to fit various types of events.

Event Planning: The hotel's dedicated events team is available to assist with planning and coordinating meetings, conferences, and private events.

Basic Facilities and Amenities

Rooms: The Thief offers a range of luxurious rooms and suites, all featuring modern amenities, including high-speed Wi-Fi, flat-screen TVs, minibars, and designer toiletries.

Dining: The hotel's restaurant, **The Thief Restaurant**, serves gourmet meals with a focus on local and international cuisine. Guests can enjoy breakfast, lunch, and dinner in a stylish setting.

Concierge Service: The concierge team is available to assist with reservations, recommendations, and other guest needs.

Business Center: A fully equipped business center is available for guests needing to work during their stay.

Opening and Closing Hours

Reception: 24 hours a day

Restaurants and Bars: Typically open from morning until late evening; exact hours may vary

Spa: Usually open from early morning to early evening; booking in advance is recommended

Price

Rates: The cost per night at The Thief typically ranges from €300 to €600, depending on the room type, season, and availability. Special packages and promotions may also be available.

Pros

Prime Location: Located near major attractions, restaurants, and waterfront views.

Luxury and Comfort: High-end amenities and stylish design enhance the guest experience.

Exceptional Service: Known for attentive and professional service.

Artistic Ambiance: A unique atmosphere with curated art and modern design.

Cons

Price: On the higher end of the spectrum, which might not be suitable for all budgets.

Busy Area: Proximity to popular areas can mean more foot traffic and occasional noise.

Local Tips

Explore Tjuvholmen: Take advantage of the hotel's location to explore the nearby Tjuvholmen district, known for its modern architecture and cultural institutions.

Reservations: Make dining and spa reservations well in advance, especially during peak seasons.

Public Transport: Utilize Oslo's efficient public transport system for easy access to other parts of the city.

2. **Hotel Continental**

Hotel Continental is a classic five-star hotel that combines historic charm with modern luxury. Located in a prime position in Oslo, it has been a favorite among royalty, celebrities, and discerning travelers for over a century. The hotel is celebrated for its sophisticated ambiance and personalized service.

Location

Address: Stortingsgata 24/26, 0161 Oslo, Norway

Proximity:

Oslo City Hall: 5 minutes by foot

Karl Johans Gate: 5 minutes by foot

The Royal Palace: 10 minutes by foot

Aker Brygge: 15-20 minutes by foot

Highlights

Historical Significance: Established in 1900, Hotel Continental has a long-standing reputation for luxury and has hosted numerous high-profile guests.

Elegant Design: The hotel features classic interiors with a blend of traditional and contemporary styles, including opulent furnishings and fine art.

Spa and Wellness

Spa: While Hotel Continental does not have an in-house spa, it offers access to nearby wellness facilities and can assist with arranging spa appointments for guests.

Fitness: The hotel has a well-equipped fitness center available to guests.

Bars

Theatercaféen: Located within the hotel, this historic café and bar is renowned for its classic ambiance and is a popular spot for enjoying drinks and light meals. The venue has been a cultural hub in Oslo for many years.

Bar: The hotel's bar area offers a refined setting for enjoying cocktails, wines, and other beverages in a sophisticated atmosphere.

Events and Conferences

Meeting Facilities: Hotel Continental offers a range of meeting rooms and event spaces, equipped with modern technology. The elegant settings are suitable for conferences, meetings, and private events.

Event Planning: The hotel's event team is experienced in organizing various types of functions and can assist with all aspects of event planning and execution.

Basic Facilities and Amenities

Rooms: The hotel boasts luxurious rooms and suites with traditional decor, high-quality furnishings, and modern amenities, including high-speed Wi-Fi, flat-screen TVs, minibars, and premium toiletries.

Dining: In addition to Theatercaféen, the hotel offers fine dining options with a focus on Norwegian and international cuisine.

Concierge Service: The concierge team is available to assist with guest requests, including reservations, sightseeing recommendations, and special arrangements.

Business Center: A fully equipped business center is available for guests needing to work during their stay.

Opening and Closing Hours

Reception: 24 hours a day

Restaurants and Bars: Typically open for breakfast, lunch, and dinner, with specific hours varying. The Theatercaféen is open daily.

Fitness Center: Usually accessible during the hotel's operational hours.

Price

Rates: Prices at Hotel Continental generally range from €250 to €500 per night, depending on the room type, season, and availability. Special offers and packages may be available.

Pros

Prime Location: Centrally located, providing easy access to major attractions, shopping, and dining.

Historical Charm: Offers a blend of historic elegance and modern luxury.

Personalized Service: Renowned for its high level of service and attention to detail.

Cultural Hub: The Theatercaféen adds a unique cultural element to the stay.

Cons

Price: On the higher end of the price spectrum, which might not fit all budgets.

No In-House Spa: Lacks a dedicated spa facility, though access to nearby wellness options is available.

Local Tips

Explore Nearby Attractions: Take advantage of the hotel's central location to explore nearby landmarks, including the Oslo City Hall and the Royal Palace.

Dining Reservations: Consider making reservations for dinner at Theatercaféen, especially during peak dining times or special occasions.

Public Transport: Utilize Oslo's efficient public transport system for convenient travel around the city.

3. Grand Hotel Oslo

Grand Hotel Oslo combines classic elegance with modern luxury. Established in 1874, the hotel has a rich history of hosting royalty, celebrities, and dignitaries. Its central location and opulent design make it a standout choice for travelers seeking a premium experience in Oslo.

Location

Address: Karl Johans gate 31, 0159 Oslo, Norway

Proximity:

Oslo Central Station: 5 minutes by foot

The Royal Palace: 10 minutes by foot

Aker Brygge: 15-20 minutes by foot

The National Gallery: 10 minutes by foot

Highlights

Historic Charm: With over a century of history, the hotel boasts a classic, elegant design, combining traditional opulence with modern amenities.

Exclusive Atmosphere: The hotel's grandeur and luxurious decor create an exclusive and sophisticated atmosphere.

Spa and Wellness

Spa: The hotel offers a wellness area with a focus on relaxation and rejuvenation. Facilities include a sauna and a relaxation area, though it does not have a full-service spa.

Fitness: The hotel features a well-equipped fitness center for guests to maintain their workout routine.

Bars

The Grand Lounge: A luxurious space where guests can enjoy afternoon tea, light snacks, and beverages in an elegant setting.

The Grand Café: A historic venue within the hotel, offering a refined ambiance for cocktails, wines, and classic Norwegian dishes.

Events and Conferences

Meeting Facilities: Grand Hotel Oslo offers a range of meeting rooms and event spaces, suitable for conferences, banquets, and private events. These spaces are equipped with modern technology and elegant furnishings.

Event Planning: The hotel's experienced events team can assist with planning and executing various events, ensuring a seamless experience.

Basic Facilities and Amenities

Rooms: The hotel offers a selection of luxurious rooms and suites, featuring high-end furnishings, elegant decor, and modern amenities such as high-speed Wi-Fi, flat-screen TVs, minibars, and premium toiletries.

Dining: In addition to The Grand Café, the hotel has a fine dining restaurant offering gourmet meals with a focus on Norwegian and international cuisine.

Concierge Service: The concierge team provides personalized assistance with reservations, sightseeing, and special requests.

Business Center: A fully equipped business center is available for guests needing to conduct business during their stay.

Opening and Closing Hours

Reception: 24 hours a day

Restaurants and Bars: Typically open for breakfast, lunch, and dinner, with specific hours varying. The Grand Café is open daily.

Fitness Center: Usually accessible during the hotel's operational hours.

Price

Rates: Prices at Grand Hotel Oslo typically range from €300 to €600 per night, depending on the room type, season, and availability. Special packages and promotions may be available.

Pros

Prime Location: Centrally located, providing easy access to major attractions, shopping, and dining.

Historical Elegance: Offers a blend of historic charm and modern luxury.

Exceptional Service: Known for its high level of personalized service and attention to detail.

Exclusive Atmosphere: The hotel's grandeur and elegance create a unique and sophisticated experience.

Cons

Price: On the higher end of the price spectrum, which might not fit all budgets.

Limited Spa Facilities: While the hotel offers wellness amenities, it does not have a full-service spa.

Local Tips

Explore Nearby: Use the hotel's central location to visit nearby landmarks like the Royal Palace and the National Gallery.

Dining Reservations: Make reservations in advance for dining at The Grand Café, particularly during busy periods.

Public Transport: Take advantage of Oslo's efficient public transport system for easy travel around the city.

4. Radisson Blu Plaza Hotel

Radisson Blu Plaza Hotel stands out for its sleek, contemporary design and extensive facilities. As one of the tallest buildings in Oslo, it offers impressive city views and provides a high standard of comfort and convenience for both leisure and business travelers.

Location

Address: Sonja Henies Plass 3, 0185 Oslo, Norway

Proximity:

Oslo Central Station: Directly adjacent, providing easy access to train, bus, and tram services.

Oslo Opera House: About 10-15 minutes by foot.

Karl Johans Gate: 5-10 minutes by foot.

The Royal Palace: Approximately 15 minutes by foot.

Highlights

Skyline Views: The hotel's location in one of Oslo's tallest buildings offers panoramic views of the city and the Oslofjord.

Modern Design: The hotel features a contemporary design with stylish interiors and high-quality finishes.

Spa and Wellness

Spa: The hotel does not have a full-service spa, but it features a wellness center with a sauna and fitness facilities.

Fitness: The hotel's fitness center is well-equipped with modern exercise machines and free weights, catering to guests who wish to maintain their workout routine.

Bars

Atrium Bar: Located in the hotel's spacious atrium, this bar offers a range of beverages, including cocktails, wines, and light snacks in a relaxed and stylish setting.

Restaurant and Bar: The hotel's restaurant, **The Summit**, located on one of the top floors, provides a refined dining experience with panoramic views of Oslo.

Events and Conferences

Meeting Facilities: Radisson Blu Plaza Hotel offers extensive meeting and conference facilities, including several flexible event rooms and a large ballroom. These spaces are equipped with state-of-the-art audiovisual technology.

Event Planning: The hotel's dedicated event team assists with planning and executing various types of events, from business meetings to private celebrations.

Basic Facilities and Amenities

Rooms: The hotel offers a range of modern and comfortable rooms and suites, equipped with amenities such as high-speed Wi-Fi, flat-screen TVs, minibars, and coffee makers.

Dining: In addition to The Summit restaurant, the hotel offers breakfast and room service options. The dining facilities cater to various tastes and preferences.

Concierge Service: The concierge team provides assistance with reservations, local recommendations, and special requests.

Business Center: A fully equipped business center is available for guests needing to conduct business during their stay.

Opening and Closing Hours

Reception: 24 hours a day

Restaurants and Bars: Typically open for breakfast, lunch, and dinner, with specific hours varying. The Atrium Bar and The Summit restaurant have extended hours.

Fitness Center: Generally accessible throughout the day, with specific hours typically outlined at check-in.

Price

Rates: Rates at Radisson Blu Plaza Hotel generally range from €200 to €400 per night, depending on the room type, season, and availability. Special offers and packages may be available.

Pros

Prime Location: Central location with easy access to transport links and major attractions.

Modern Amenities: Offers contemporary facilities and stylish design.

Stunning Views: High floors provide panoramic views of Oslo.

Extensive Facilities: Comprehensive meeting and event facilities.

Cons

Price: Can be on the higher side, which might not suit all budgets.

Lack of Full-Service Spa: While wellness facilities are available, the hotel does not have a full-service spa.

Local Tips

Explore Nearby: Use the hotel's proximity to the central station and main attractions to explore Oslo's cultural and shopping districts.

Dining Reservations: Consider making reservations at The Summit restaurant, especially for dinner, to ensure a table with a view.

Public Transport: The adjacent central station makes it easy to travel to other parts of Oslo and beyond.

The Ultimate Oslo Travel Guide (2025 Edition)

5. Frogner House Apartments – Skovveien 8

Frogner House Apartments – Skovveien 8 provides serviced apartments in the Frogner district, known for its residential charm and proximity to central Oslo. These apartments are designed to offer a home-like atmosphere with the convenience of hotel services, ideal for both short and long-term stays.

Location

Address: Skovveien 8, 0257 Oslo, Norway

Proximity:

Frogner Park: 5-10 minutes by foot, home to the Vigeland Sculpture Park.

Karl Johans Gate: About 15-20 minutes by public transport or a 25-minute walk.

Oslo City Center: 15-20 minutes by public transport or a 25-minute walk.

Aker Brygge: Around 20 minutes by public transport or a 30-minute walk.

Highlights

Residential Comfort: Offers a more home-like environment with self-catering facilities, making it suitable for longer stays or those preferring more independence.

Convenience: Located in a pleasant residential area with easy access to Oslo's main attractions and amenities.

Rooms and Amenities

Apartments: The property offers a range of fully furnished apartments, including studio, one-bedroom, and two-bedroom options. Each apartment is equipped with:

Kitchen: Fully equipped kitchens or kitchenettes with essential appliances and utensils.

Living Space: Comfortable living areas with seating, dining tables, and often workspaces.

Bedrooms: Cozy and well-furnished bedrooms with high-quality bedding.

Bathrooms: Private bathrooms with modern fixtures and complimentary toiletries.

Wi-Fi: High-speed internet is available throughout the property.

Basic Facilities and Amenities

Self-Catering: Apartments come with kitchen facilities, allowing guests to prepare their own meals.

Housekeeping: Regular housekeeping services are provided, with more frequent services available upon request.

Laundry: Some apartments may offer laundry facilities, or guests can access a shared laundry room.

Concierge Service: Limited concierge services are available, but staff can assist with local recommendations and arrangements.

Opening and Closing Hours

Reception: The reception is typically open during business hours, but self-check-in options may be available for guests arriving outside these hours. Specific hours should be confirmed with the property prior to arrival.

Check-In/Check-Out: Check-in times are generally in the afternoon (e.g., from 3 PM), and check-out is usually by midday (e.g., 11 AM). Early check-ins and late check-outs may be arranged based on availability.

Price

Rates: Prices at Frogner House Apartments – Skovveien 8 vary depending on the season, apartment type, and length of stay. Rates generally range from €100 to €250 per night, with discounts available for longer stays.

Pros

Home-Like Environment: Offers the comfort and flexibility of self-catering with a more residential feel.

Good Location: Situated in a charming neighborhood with easy access to public transport and attractions.

Comfortable and Well-Equipped: Provides spacious and well-furnished accommodations with modern amenities.

Cons

Limited Hotel Services: While offering self-catering facilities, it lacks some of the services and amenities of a full-service hotel.

Distance from Central Attractions: Although not far from the city center, it may be a bit of a walk or a short transit ride to reach some of Oslo's main attractions.

Local Tips

Explore Frogner: Take the time to explore the Frogner area, known for its beautiful parks, charming streets, and local cafes.

Public Transport: Use Oslo's efficient public transport system to easily reach the city center and other areas of interest.

Local Amenities: Check out local grocery stores and markets in the Frogner neighborhood for fresh produce and essentials.

The Ultimate Oslo Travel Guide (2025 Edition)

Mid-Range Hotels

For travelers seeking comfort and quality without breaking the bank, Oslo's mid-range hotels offer an excellent balance of affordability and amenities. These hotels provide stylish rooms, reliable services, and convenient locations, making them ideal for both short and extended stays. Enjoy modern comforts, friendly service, and a central base from which to explore Oslo's attractions and vibrant neighborhoods.

Top 5 Mid-Range Hotels

1. **Comfort Hotel Xpress Central Station**

Comfort Hotel Xpress Central Station is a contemporary hotel that emphasizes a straightforward, no-frills approach while delivering essential comforts. Its central location and modern design make it a practical choice for both business and leisure travelers seeking easy access to Oslo's main attractions and transportation options.

Location

Address: Skippergata 1A, 0152 Oslo, Norway

Proximity:

Oslo Central Station: Directly adjacent, offering immediate access to trains, buses, and trams.

Karl Johans Gate: Approximately 5 minutes by foot.

Oslo Opera House: About 10 minutes by foot.

The Royal Palace: Around 15 minutes by foot.

Highlights

Convenient Location: The hotel's proximity to Oslo Central Station and major attractions makes it highly convenient for travelers.

Modern Design: Features a sleek, contemporary design with a focus on clean lines and functional spaces.

Self-Service Model: Emphasizes a self-service approach, allowing guests to manage their stay with ease.

Spa and Wellness

Spa: The hotel does not have an on-site spa or wellness center. However, guests can access nearby fitness centers or wellness facilities in Oslo.

Fitness: While there is no gym on-site, guests can often find partnerships with local fitness centers or use the surrounding area for jogging and walking.

Bars

Bar: Comfort Hotel Xpress Central Station does not have a bar on the premises. Guests can explore nearby bars and cafes in the vibrant city center for a variety of drinking and dining options.

Events and Conferences

Meeting Facilities: The hotel does not offer dedicated conference or meeting rooms. For business travelers requiring meeting spaces, nearby venues or conference centers would need to be utilized.

Basic Facilities and Amenities

Rooms: The hotel offers a range of modern rooms equipped with:

Comfortable Bedding: Quality beds with hypoallergenic pillows.

Technology: Free Wi-Fi, flat-screen TVs, and convenient power outlets.

Workspaces: Desks and ergonomic chairs for business travelers.

Bathrooms: Private bathrooms with basic amenities, including a shower and toiletries.

Self-Service: The hotel features a self-service concept, where guests handle check-in/check-out and other services using kiosks.

Breakfast: The hotel offers a breakfast buffet with a variety of options, including continental and Scandinavian favorites.

Opening and Closing Hours

Reception: 24 hours a day, providing flexibility for check-in and check-out.

Breakfast: Typically served from early morning until mid-morning; exact hours may vary.

Check-In/Check-Out: Check-in is usually from 3 PM, and check-out is by 11 AM. Early check-ins and late check-outs may be arranged based on availability.

Price

Rates: Prices at Comfort Hotel Xpress Central Station generally range from €100 to €200 per night, depending on the season, room type, and booking time. Rates are often competitive for the central location and modern amenities.

Pros

Prime Location: Directly next to Oslo Central Station and close to major attractions, making it convenient for exploring the city and traveling.

Modern and Clean: Offers a contemporary design with well-maintained facilities.

Affordability: Provides good value for money, especially considering its central location.

24-Hour Reception: Flexible check-in and check-out times accommodate various travel schedules.

Cons

Limited Amenities: Lacks some amenities such as a spa, bar, and dedicated meeting facilities.

Basic Services: The self-service model might not suit travelers looking for more personalized services or extensive hotel facilities.

Local Tips

Explore Nearby: Take advantage of the hotel's central location to explore nearby attractions like the Oslo Opera House, Karl Johans Gate, and the Royal Palace.

Public Transport: Use the nearby Oslo Central Station for easy access to trains, buses, and trams, making it simple to explore the city and surrounding areas.

Dining: Discover local cafes and restaurants in the vicinity of the hotel for diverse dining options, from casual bites to fine dining experiences.

2. Scandic Byporten

Scandic Byporten offers contemporary accommodations with a focus on practicality and guest satisfaction. It's part of the Scandic chain, which is known for its consistent quality and service. The hotel is particularly noted for its central location and modern design.

Location

Address: Jernbanetorget 6, 0154 Oslo, Norway

Proximity:

Oslo Central Station: Directly adjacent, providing easy access to trains, buses, and trams.

Karl Johans Gate: About 5 minutes by foot.

Oslo Opera House: Approximately 10 minutes by foot.

Aker Brygge: Around 15-20 minutes by foot.

Highlights

Central Location: Located right next to Oslo Central Station, making it highly convenient for transportation and exploring the city.

Modern Design: Features contemporary interiors with a focus on comfort and functionality.

Shopping and Dining: Situated within Byporten Shopping Center, providing easy access to retail stores, restaurants, and cafes.

Spa and Wellness

Spa: The hotel does not have an on-site spa. However, guests can find wellness centers and gyms nearby.

Fitness: The hotel offers a fitness center with modern equipment for guests looking to maintain their workout routine during their stay.

Bars

Bar: The hotel does not have a dedicated bar, but guests can enjoy drinks and light snacks in the hotel's common areas or visit nearby bars and cafes in the Byporten Shopping Center.

Events and Conferences

Meeting Facilities: Scandic Byporten provides meeting and event spaces equipped with modern audiovisual technology. The hotel offers a range of meeting rooms suitable for small to medium-sized gatherings.

Event Planning: The hotel's event team assists with planning and organizing meetings, conferences, and other events.

Basic Facilities and Amenities

Rooms: The hotel offers a variety of modern rooms, including:

Comfortable Bedding: High-quality beds and bedding for a restful stay.

Technology: Free Wi-Fi, flat-screen TVs, and convenient power outlets.

Workspaces: Desks and ergonomic chairs for business travelers.

Bathrooms: Private bathrooms with modern fixtures and complimentary toiletries.

Dining: A breakfast buffet is available each morning, featuring a range of options including Scandinavian and international dishes. The hotel may also offer light meals and snacks throughout the day.

Concierge Service: The hotel's staff can assist with local recommendations, reservations, and other guest needs.

Opening and Closing Hours

Reception: 24 hours a day, providing flexibility for check-in and check-out.

Breakfast: Typically served from early morning until mid-morning; exact hours may vary.

Fitness Center: Generally accessible throughout the day, with specific hours typically outlined at check-in.

Price

Rates: Prices at Scandic Byporten generally range from €150 to €250 per night, depending on the room type, season, and booking time. Rates are competitive for a hotel in such a central location.

Pros

Prime Location: Directly next to Oslo Central Station and close to major attractions, shopping, and dining options.

Modern and Comfortable: Offers contemporary design and well-maintained facilities.

Good Value: Provides a high level of comfort and convenience for a mid-range price.

24-Hour Reception: Flexible check-in and check-out times accommodate various travel schedules.

Cons

Limited Amenities: Lacks some amenities such as an on-site spa and dedicated bar.

Basic Services: The hotel's focus on practicality may result in fewer personalized services compared to higher-end hotels.

Local Tips

Explore Nearby: Use the hotel's central location to visit nearby landmarks like the Oslo Opera House and Karl Johans Gate.

Shopping and Dining: Take advantage of the Byporten Shopping Center for convenient shopping and dining options.

Public Transport: Utilize the adjacent Oslo Central Station for easy access to other parts of Oslo and beyond.

3. **Thon Hotel Munch**

Thon Hotel Munch is part of the Thon Hotels chain, known for its quality and value. The hotel offers a relaxed atmosphere with modern accommodations, making it suitable for both business and leisure travelers.

Location

Address: Munchs gate 5, 0165 Oslo, Norway

Proximity:

Karl Johans Gate: About 10 minutes by foot.

Oslo Central Station: Approximately 15 minutes by foot.

The Royal Palace: Around 15 minutes by foot.

Aker Brygge: Around 20 minutes by foot or a short tram ride.

Highlights

Central Location: Situated in a convenient area for exploring Oslo's main attractions and accessing public transport.

Modern Design: Offers contemporary rooms and facilities with a focus on comfort and functionality.

Value for Money: Provides a good balance of quality and affordability.

Spa and Wellness

Spa: Thon Hotel Munch does not have an on-site spa. However, guests can access nearby fitness centers or wellness facilities in Oslo.

Fitness: The hotel features a small fitness center equipped with basic exercise machines and free weights.

Bars

Bar: The hotel does not have a dedicated bar. However, guests can explore nearby bars and cafes for a variety of drinking and dining options.

Events and Conferences

Meeting Facilities: The hotel does not offer dedicated conference or meeting rooms. For business events or meetings, nearby venues or conference centers may be utilized.

Basic Facilities and Amenities

Rooms: The hotel offers a variety of modern rooms, including:

Comfortable Bedding: Quality beds and linens for a restful stay.

Technology: Free Wi-Fi, flat-screen TVs, and convenient power outlets.

Workspaces: Desks and ergonomic chairs for business travelers.

Bathrooms: Private bathrooms with modern fixtures and complimentary toiletries.

Dining: A buffet breakfast is served each morning with a selection of hot and cold items. The hotel may also provide light snacks and refreshments throughout the day.

Concierge Service: The hotel's staff can assist with local recommendations, reservations, and other guest needs.

Opening and Closing Hours

Reception: 24 hours a day, providing flexibility for check-in and check-out.

Breakfast: Typically served from early morning until mid-morning; exact hours may vary.

Fitness Center: Generally accessible throughout the day, with specific hours typically outlined at check-in.

Price

Rates: Prices at Thon Hotel Munch generally range from €120 to €200 per night, depending on the room type, season, and booking time. Rates are competitive for a mid-range hotel in a central location.

Pros

Good Location: Central location allows for easy access to major attractions, public transport, and dining options.

Modern and Comfortable: Offers contemporary design and well-maintained facilities.

Affordability: Provides good value for money, especially considering its location and amenities.

24-Hour Reception: Flexible check-in and check-out times accommodate various travel schedules.

Cons

Limited Amenities: Lacks some amenities such as a spa and dedicated bar.

Basic Services: The hotel's focus on practicality might result in fewer personalized services compared to higher-end hotels.

Local Tips

Explore the Area: Take advantage of the hotel's location to explore nearby attractions such as Karl Johans Gate, the Royal Palace, and the Oslo Opera House.

Public Transport: Use nearby tram and bus stops for easy travel around Oslo and to reach other parts of the city.

Local Dining: Discover local cafes and restaurants in the area for a variety of dining options, from casual meals to fine dining.

4. Radisson Blu Scandinavia Hotel

Radisson Blu Scandinavia Hotel is a contemporary hotel that combines luxury with practicality, catering to both business and leisure travelers. It is part of the Radisson Blu chain, known for its consistent quality and high standards of service.

Location

Address: Holbergs gate 30, 0166 Oslo, Norway

Proximity:

Karl Johans Gate: About 10 minutes by foot.

Oslo Central Station: Approximately 15 minutes by foot.

The Royal Palace: Around 10 minutes by foot.

Oslo Opera House: Approximately 20 minutes by foot.

Highlights

Central Location: Located in the heart of Oslo, providing easy access to major attractions, shopping, and dining.

Modern Amenities: Offers a wide range of modern amenities and facilities, ensuring a comfortable and convenient stay.

Stunning Views: Some rooms and public areas offer panoramic views of Oslo and the Oslofjord.

Spa and Wellness

Spa: The hotel features a wellness area that includes a spa and fitness center. The spa offers a range of treatments, including massages and beauty services.

Fitness: The hotel's fitness center is well-equipped with modern exercise machines, free weights, and a sauna.

Bars

SkyBar: Located on the top floor, this stylish bar offers stunning views of Oslo and a selection of cocktails, wines, and light snacks.

Brasserie: The hotel's dining venue provides a relaxed atmosphere for breakfast, lunch, and dinner, featuring a variety of international and local dishes.

Events and Conferences

Meeting Facilities: Radisson Blu Scandinavia Hotel has extensive conference and meeting facilities, including a large ballroom and several meeting rooms. These spaces are equipped with state-of-the-art audiovisual technology and can accommodate various event sizes.

Event Planning: The hotel's event team provides support with planning and executing meetings, conferences, and other events, ensuring a seamless experience.

Basic Facilities and Amenities

Rooms: The hotel offers a range of luxurious rooms and suites, featuring:

Comfortable Bedding: High-quality beds and linens.

Technology: Free high-speed Wi-Fi, flat-screen TVs, and in-room entertainment options.

Workspaces: Desks and ergonomic chairs for business travelers.

Bathrooms: Private bathrooms with modern fixtures, high-quality toiletries, and bathrobes.

Dining: Includes a variety of dining options, from a buffet breakfast to à la carte lunch and dinner. The hotel also offers room service.

Concierge Service: The concierge team assists with reservations, local recommendations, and special requests.

Business Center: A fully equipped business center is available for guests needing to conduct business.

Opening and Closing Hours

Reception: 24 hours a day, providing flexible check-in and check-out times.

Dining: The Brasserie is typically open for breakfast, lunch, and dinner, with specific hours varying. The SkyBar usually operates in the evening.

Fitness Center: Generally accessible throughout the day, with specific hours typically outlined at check-in.

Price

Rates: Prices at Radisson Blu Scandinavia Hotel generally range from €200 to €400 per night, depending on the room type, season, and availability. Rates can be higher during peak seasons or special events.

Pros

Prime Location: Central location with easy access to major attractions and transport links.

Luxurious Amenities: Offers a range of high-quality amenities and services, including a spa, fitness center, and dining options.

Stunning Views: Some rooms and the SkyBar offer beautiful views of Oslo and the surrounding areas.

Extensive Facilities: Features comprehensive meeting and event facilities, making it suitable for business travelers.

Cons

Price: Can be on the higher end of the price spectrum, which might not suit all budgets.

Basic Services: While luxurious, the hotel's self-service approach may lack some personalized touches compared to boutique or smaller luxury hotels.

Local Tips

Explore the Area: Use the hotel's central location to explore nearby attractions such as the Oslo Opera House, the Royal Palace, and the waterfront area of Aker Brygge.

Visit the SkyBar: Take advantage of the SkyBar for panoramic views and a relaxing drink.

Public Transport: Utilize Oslo's efficient public transport system for easy travel to other parts of the city and beyond.

5. Quality Hotel Strand Gjøa

Quality Hotel Strand Gjøa provides a welcoming atmosphere with a focus on comfort and practicality. As part of the Nordic Choice Hotels group, it emphasizes quality service and a pleasant stay experience.

Location

Address: Dronningens gate 5, 0152 Oslo, Norway

Proximity:

Karl Johans Gate: Approximately 10 minutes by foot.

Oslo Central Station: About 15 minutes by foot.

The Royal Palace: Around 15 minutes by foot.

Aker Brygge: Approximately 20 minutes by foot or a short tram ride.

Highlights

Central Location: Situated in Oslo's city center, offering easy access to major attractions, shopping, and dining options.

Comfortable Accommodations: Features well-appointed rooms with a focus on guest comfort.

Modern Amenities: Provides a range of amenities to enhance the guest experience.

Spa and Wellness

Spa: The hotel does not have an on-site spa. However, guests can find nearby wellness facilities or fitness centers in Oslo.

Fitness: The hotel features a fitness center equipped with basic exercise machines and weights for guests looking to stay active.

Bars

Bar: The hotel does not have a dedicated bar. Guests can explore nearby bars and cafes in the city center for a variety of drinking and dining options.

Events and Conferences

Meeting Facilities: Quality Hotel Strand Gjøa offers meeting and event spaces suitable for various sizes of gatherings. The facilities are equipped with modern audiovisual technology.

Event Planning: The hotel's event team provides support for planning and organizing meetings, conferences, and other events.

Basic Facilities and Amenities

Rooms: The hotel offers a range of comfortable rooms, including:

Comfortable Bedding: High-quality beds and linens.

Technology: Free Wi-Fi, flat-screen TVs, and convenient power outlets.

Workspaces: Desks and ergonomic chairs for business travelers.

Bathrooms: Private bathrooms with modern fixtures, high-quality toiletries, and bathrobes.

Dining: A buffet breakfast is available each morning, featuring a variety of options. The hotel may also offer light meals and snacks throughout the day.

Concierge Service: The hotel's staff can assist with local recommendations, reservations, and other guest needs.

Business Center: A business center with essential facilities is available for guests needing to conduct business.

Opening and Closing Hours

Reception: 24 hours a day, providing flexibility for check-in and check-out.

Dining: Breakfast is typically served from early morning until mid-morning; exact hours may vary. The availability of other meals and snacks may be limited.

Fitness Center: Generally accessible throughout the day, with specific hours outlined at check-in.

Price

Rates: Prices at Quality Hotel Strand Gjøa generally range from €120 to €200 per night, depending on the room type, season, and booking time. Rates are competitive for a mid-range hotel in a central location.

Pros

Central Location: Offers a convenient base for exploring Oslo's attractions and accessing public transport.

Comfortable Accommodations: Provides well-appointed rooms and modern amenities.

Good Value: Offers a good balance of quality and affordability for mid-range travelers.

24-Hour Reception: Flexible check-in and check-out times accommodate various travel schedules.

Cons

Limited Amenities: Lacks some amenities such as an on-site bar and spa.

Basic Services: The hotel's focus on practicality might result in fewer personalized services compared to higher-end hotels.

Local Tips

Explore the City: Use the hotel's central location to visit nearby attractions like Karl Johans Gate, the Royal Palace, and the Oslo Opera House.

Public Transport: Take advantage of the nearby tram and bus stops for easy travel around Oslo and to reach other parts of the city.

Local Dining: Discover local restaurants and cafes in the city center for a variety of dining options.

Budget Accommodation

For travelers seeking cost-effective options, Oslo offers a range of budget accommodations that provide essential comforts without a hefty price tag. These budget-friendly options include hostels, guesthouses, and budget hotels, offering clean, simple rooms and convenient locations. Enjoy affordable stays while exploring the city's attractions and vibrant neighborhoods.

Top 5 Budget Accommodation

1. **Anker Hostel**

Anker Hostel is a budget hostel offering simple, comfortable accommodations with a focus on affordability and accessibility. It is part of the Anker Hotels group, known for providing practical lodging solutions in central locations.

Location

Address: Storgata 55, 0182 Oslo, Norway

Proximity:

Oslo Central Station: About 10 minutes by foot.

Karl Johans Gate: Approximately 15 minutes by foot.

The Royal Palace: Around 20 minutes by foot.

Aker Brygge: About 25 minutes by foot or a short tram ride.

Highlights

Affordable Rates: Offers budget-friendly accommodation options, making it a good choice for cost-conscious travelers.

Central Location: Situated close to Oslo's main attractions and transport links.

Simple Accommodations: Provides basic but clean and comfortable lodging.

Spa and Wellness

Spa: Anker Hostel does not have an on-site spa or wellness facilities. Guests looking for spa treatments can explore nearby options in Oslo.

Fitness: The hostel does not have a fitness center. However, guests can find local gyms or use the surrounding area for jogging and exercise.

Bars

Bar: The hostel does not have a bar on-site. Guests can explore nearby bars, cafes, and restaurants in the city center for a variety of drinking and dining options.

Events and Conferences

Meeting Facilities: Anker Hostel does not offer dedicated meeting or conference facilities. For business travelers or those requiring event spaces, nearby venues or conference centers would be suitable.

Basic Facilities and Amenities

Rooms: The hostel offers a range of simple rooms, including:

Dormitories: Shared dormitory-style rooms with bunk beds.

Private Rooms: Basic private rooms with double or single beds.

Bedding: Provided, with shared or private bathroom facilities depending on the room type.

Common Areas: Includes common areas where guests can relax, socialize, and use shared kitchen facilities.

Kitchen: A communal kitchen is available for guests to prepare their own meals.

Wi-Fi: Free Wi-Fi is available throughout the hostel.

Luggage Storage: Luggage storage is provided for guests arriving before check-in or departing after check-out.

Opening and Closing Hours

Reception: Typically open 24 hours a day, allowing for flexible check-in and check-out times. It's advisable to confirm this with the hostel directly, as hours may vary.

Kitchen: Usually available throughout the day; specific hours may vary.

Price

Rates: Prices at Anker Hostel generally range from €30 to €70 per night, depending on the room type, season, and availability. Rates are competitive for a budget accommodation option in Oslo.

Pros

Affordable: Provides budget-friendly lodging options, ideal for cost-conscious travelers.

Central Location: Conveniently located near major attractions and public transport.

Basic Comfort: Clean and simple accommodations with essential amenities.

Communal Facilities: Includes shared kitchen and common areas for guest use.

Cons

Limited Amenities: Lacks amenities such as a bar, spa, or dedicated meeting facilities.

Basic Accommodations: Rooms and facilities are basic and may not offer the same level of comfort or service as higher-end options.

Local Tips

Explore the Area: Take advantage of the hostel's central location to visit nearby attractions such as Karl Johans Gate, the Royal Palace, and the Oslo Opera House.

Public Transport: Use nearby tram and bus stops for easy travel around Oslo and to reach other parts of the city.

Local Dining: Check out local cafes and restaurants in the vicinity for affordable dining options.

2. Oslo Hostel Central

Oslo Hostel Central offers a practical and cost-effective lodging solution in Oslo. It provides simple, clean accommodations and aims to serve budget-conscious travelers with a focus on convenience and essential services.

Location

Address: Bislettgata 4A, 0166 Oslo, Norway

Proximity:

Oslo Central Station: Approximately 15 minutes by foot or a short tram ride.

Karl Johans Gate: Around 15 minutes by foot.

The Royal Palace: About 20 minutes by foot.

Aker Brygge: Approximately 25 minutes by foot or a short tram ride.

Highlights

Budget-Friendly: Offers economical rates suitable for travelers on a budget.

Central Location: Conveniently located near major attractions and public transportation.

Simple Accommodations: Provides basic, no-frills lodging with essential amenities.

Spa and Wellness

Spa: Oslo Hostel Central does not have an on-site spa. Guests seeking spa treatments can find options in the nearby area.

Fitness: The hostel does not offer a fitness center. Local gyms or outdoor exercise options are available in Oslo.

Bars

Bar: The hostel does not have a bar. Guests can explore nearby bars, cafes, and restaurants in the city center for a variety of social and dining experiences.

Events and Conferences

Meeting Facilities: The hostel does not provide dedicated meeting or conference facilities. For business events or meetings, guests would need to use nearby venues or conference centers.

Basic Facilities and Amenities

Rooms: The hostel offers a range of room types, including:

Dormitories: Shared dormitory-style rooms with bunk beds.

Private Rooms: Basic private rooms with single or double beds.

Bedding: Provided, with shared or private bathrooms depending on the room type.

Common Areas: Includes communal areas where guests can relax and socialize.

Kitchen: A shared kitchen is available for guests to prepare their own meals.

Wi-Fi: Free Wi-Fi is available throughout the hostel.

Luggage Storage: Luggage storage facilities are available for guests before check-in or after check-out.

Opening and Closing Hours

Reception: Generally open during standard hours, but it's advisable to check with the hostel for specific times. Some hostels may have 24-hour reception.

Kitchen: Typically available throughout the day; specific hours may vary.

Price

Rates: Prices at Oslo Hostel Central typically range from €30 to €60 per night, depending on the room type, season, and availability. These rates are competitive for budget accommodation in Oslo.

Pros

Affordable: Provides budget-friendly lodging options for cost-conscious travelers.

Central Location: Conveniently situated near key attractions and public transport.

Basic Comfort: Clean and straightforward accommodations with necessary amenities.

Shared Facilities: Includes communal kitchen and common areas for guest use.

Cons

Limited Amenities: Lacks amenities such as a bar, spa, or conference facilities.

Basic Accommodations: Rooms and facilities are basic and may not offer the same level of comfort or service as higher-end options.

Local Tips

Explore Nearby: Use the hostel's central location to visit nearby attractions like Karl Johans Gate, the Royal Palace, and the Oslo Opera House.

Public Transport: Utilize the nearby tram and bus stops for convenient travel around Oslo and to reach other parts of the city.

Local Dining: Check out local cafes and restaurants in the vicinity for affordable dining options.

Grace Bennett

3. Citybox Oslo

Citybox Oslo caters to travelers looking for affordable, self-service accommodations in a central location. The hotel focuses on providing a clean, comfortable environment with minimalistic design and essential amenities.

Location

Address: Prinsens gate 6, 0152 Oslo, Norway

Proximity:

Oslo Central Station: About 10 minutes by foot.

Karl Johans Gate: Approximately 5 minutes by foot.

The Royal Palace: Around 15 minutes by foot.

Aker Brygge: Approximately 20 minutes by foot or a short tram ride.

Highlights

Affordable Rates: Offers budget-friendly pricing, making it a great choice for cost-conscious travelers.

Self-Service Concept: Focuses on a streamlined check-in/check-out process with minimal staff interaction.

Modern Design: Features contemporary and functional design elements.

Spa and Wellness

Spa: Citybox Oslo does not have an on-site spa. Guests can explore local wellness centers or spas in Oslo for relaxation and treatments.

Fitness: The hotel does not offer a fitness center. Nearby gyms or outdoor spaces are available for exercise.

Bars

Bar: The hotel does not have an on-site bar. Guests can visit nearby bars, cafes, and restaurants in Oslo for socializing and dining.

Events and Conferences

Meeting Facilities: Citybox Oslo does not provide dedicated meeting or conference rooms. For business meetings or events, guests will need to use nearby venues or conference centers.

Basic Facilities and Amenities

Rooms: The hotel offers a variety of modern rooms, including:

Standard Rooms: Clean, simple rooms with basic furnishings.

Comfort: Includes comfortable beds, free Wi-Fi, and flat-screen TVs.

Bathrooms: Private bathrooms with modern fixtures and complimentary toiletries.

Self-Service Check-In/Check-Out: Automated kiosks are available for easy check-in and check-out.

Common Areas: Includes a lounge area where guests can relax and socialize.

Kitchen: A shared kitchen is available for guests to prepare their own meals.

Luggage Storage: Luggage storage facilities are available for guests before check-in or after check-out.

Opening and Closing Hours

Reception: Citybox Oslo operates with a self-service model, meaning there is no traditional reception desk. Check-in and check-out are managed through automated kiosks.

Kitchen: The shared kitchen is available throughout the day; specific hours may vary.

Price

Rates: Prices at Citybox Oslo typically range from €80 to €150 per night, depending on the room type, season, and availability. Rates are competitive for a mid-range hotel in a central location.

Pros

Affordable: Provides budget-friendly accommodation options with modern amenities.

Central Location: Conveniently located near major attractions and public transport.

Self-Service Convenience: Streamlined check-in and check-out process.

Modern and Clean: Features contemporary design and well-maintained facilities.

Cons

Limited Services: Lacks traditional hotel services such as a bar, spa, or full-service restaurant.

Basic Accommodations: Rooms and facilities are functional but minimalistic.

Local Tips

Explore the City: Utilize the hotel's central location to visit nearby attractions such as Karl Johans Gate, the Royal Palace, and the Oslo Opera House.

Public Transport: Take advantage of the nearby tram and bus stops for easy travel around Oslo.

Local Dining: Discover local cafes and restaurants in the vicinity for a variety of dining options.

4. Smarthotel Oslo

Smarthotel Oslo is designed to provide affordable and efficient accommodations for travelers seeking comfort without extra frills. The hotel emphasizes practicality and simplicity, making it a good choice for budget-conscious guests.

Location

Address: St. Olavs Gate 26, 0166 Oslo, Norway

Proximity:

Oslo Central Station: About 10 minutes by foot.

Karl Johans Gate: Approximately 10 minutes by foot.

The Royal Palace: Around 15 minutes by foot.

Aker Brygge: Approximately 20 minutes by foot or a short tram ride.

Highlights

Affordable Rates: Offers budget-friendly pricing with a focus on delivering good value for money.

Modern and Functional: Features a contemporary design with a practical approach to accommodations.

Central Location: Conveniently located near major attractions and public transport.

Spa and Wellness

Spa: Smarthotel Oslo does not have an on-site spa. Guests seeking spa treatments can find options in the surrounding area.

Fitness: The hotel does not offer a fitness center. Local gyms or outdoor spaces are available for exercise.

Bars

Bar: The hotel does not have a bar on-site. Guests can explore nearby bars, cafes, and restaurants in the city center for socializing and dining.

Events and Conferences

Meeting Facilities: Smarthotel Oslo does not provide dedicated meeting or conference rooms. For business meetings or events, nearby venues or conference centers would be suitable.

Basic Facilities and Amenities

Rooms: The hotel offers a range of simple, modern rooms, including:

Standard Rooms: Basic yet comfortable rooms with essential furnishings.

Bedding: High-quality beds and linens for a restful stay.

Technology: Free Wi-Fi and flat-screen TVs.

Bathrooms: Private bathrooms with modern fixtures and complimentary toiletries.

Common Areas: Includes a lounge area where guests can relax and socialize.

Breakfast: A buffet breakfast is typically available, offering a variety of options to start the day.

Concierge Service: The staff can assist with local recommendations and reservations.

Opening and Closing Hours

Reception: Typically open during standard hours. Specific times may vary, so it's advisable to check directly with the hotel.

Breakfast: Served in the morning, with hours usually extending from early morning to mid-morning.

Common Areas: Accessible throughout the day.

Price

Rates: Prices at Smarthotel Oslo generally range from €80 to €150 per night, depending on the room type, season, and availability. Rates are competitive for budget accommodations in a central location.

Pros

Affordable: Provides cost-effective lodging options with modern amenities.

Central Location: Situated near key attractions and transport links, making it convenient for exploring Oslo.

Clean and Modern: Features contemporary design and well-maintained facilities.

Breakfast Included: Offers a buffet breakfast, adding value to the stay.

Cons

Limited Amenities: Lacks amenities such as a bar, spa, or full-service restaurant.

Basic Accommodations: Rooms and facilities are functional but minimalistic.

Local Tips

Explore Nearby: Take advantage of the hotel's central location to visit nearby attractions like Karl Johans Gate, the Royal Palace, and the Oslo Opera House.

Public Transport: Use nearby tram and bus stops for easy travel around Oslo and to reach other parts of the city.

Local Dining: Discover local cafes and restaurants in the vicinity for a variety of dining options.

5. Cochs Pensjonat

Cochs Pensjonat is a charming and practical guesthouse offering a cozy and budget-friendly stay in Oslo. It is popular among travelers for its welcoming atmosphere and value-for-money accommodations.

Location

Address: Bislettgata 8, 0169 Oslo, Norway

Proximity:

Oslo Central Station: About 15 minutes by foot or a short tram ride.

Karl Johans Gate: Approximately 15 minutes by foot.

The Royal Palace: Around 20 minutes by foot.

Aker Brygge: Approximately 25 minutes by foot or a short tram ride.

Highlights

Affordable Rates: Provides budget-friendly accommodation options that offer good value for money.

Charming Atmosphere: Features a warm and inviting environment with a more personal touch compared to larger hotels.

Central Location: Located in a central area with easy access to major attractions and public transportation.

Spa and Wellness

Spa: Cochs Pensjonat does not have an on-site spa. Guests looking for spa treatments can explore nearby wellness centers in Oslo.

Fitness: The guesthouse does not have a fitness center. Nearby gyms or outdoor areas are available for exercise.

Bars

Bar: The guesthouse does not have an on-site bar. Guests can explore local bars and cafes in the vicinity for drinks and socializing.

Events and Conferences

Meeting Facilities: Cochs Pensjonat does not offer dedicated meeting or conference facilities. For business meetings or events, guests would need to use nearby venues or conference centers.

Basic Facilities and Amenities

Rooms: The guesthouse offers a range of simple yet comfortable rooms, including:

Single and Double Rooms: Basic rooms with essential furnishings.

Bedding: Comfortable beds and clean linens.

Technology: Free Wi-Fi and sometimes flat-screen TVs.

Bathrooms: Private or shared bathrooms depending on the room type, with modern fixtures and complimentary toiletries.

Common Areas: Includes common areas where guests can relax and socialize.

Breakfast: A continental breakfast may be available, providing a simple start to the day.

Concierge Service: The staff can assist with local recommendations and reservations.

Opening and Closing Hours

Reception: Generally open during standard hours. It's best to confirm specific times directly with the guesthouse.

Breakfast: Typically served in the morning, with hours extending from early to mid-morning.

Common Areas: Accessible throughout the day.

Price

Rates: Prices at Cochs Pensjonat generally range from €60 to €120 per night, depending on the room type, season, and availability. Rates are competitive for budget accommodations in Oslo.

Pros

Affordable: Offers budget-friendly pricing with comfortable and clean accommodations.

Central Location: Conveniently located near key attractions and public transport.

Charming and Personal: Provides a more intimate and personal lodging experience.

Breakfast Included: Continental breakfast adds value to the stay.

Cons

Limited Amenities: Lacks on-site facilities such as a bar or spa.

Basic Accommodations: Rooms and services are functional but minimalistic.

Local Tips

Explore the Area: Use the guesthouse's central location to visit nearby attractions like Karl Johans Gate, the Royal Palace, and the Oslo Opera House.

Public Transport: Utilize nearby tram and bus stops for convenient travel around Oslo and to explore other parts of the city.

Local Dining: Discover local cafes and restaurants in the area for a variety of dining options.

Hostels

Hostels in Oslo provide budget-friendly accommodations with a social atmosphere, perfect for travelers looking to save on costs while meeting fellow adventurers. These hostels offer a range of options from dormitory-style rooms to private spaces, featuring shared amenities like kitchens and common areas. Enjoy affordable stays and a vibrant community experience in Oslo.

Top 5 Hostels

1. Anker Hostel

Anker Hostel offers budget-friendly accommodations in a central location, catering to travelers who seek a cost-effective place to stay without sacrificing accessibility and comfort. The hostel provides basic amenities with a focus on practicality and convenience.

Location

Address: Storgata 55, 0182 Oslo, Norway

Proximity:

Oslo Central Station: About 15 minutes by foot or a short tram ride.

Karl Johans Gate: Approximately 10 minutes by foot.

The Royal Palace: Around 20 minutes by foot.

Aker Brygge: About 25 minutes by foot or a short tram ride.

Highlights

Affordable Rates: Offers budget-friendly prices that cater to travelers seeking economical options.

Central Location: Conveniently situated close to Oslo's main attractions and public transportation.

Simple Accommodations: Provides straightforward, clean, and functional lodging.

Spa and Wellness

Spa: Anker Hostel does not have an on-site spa. Guests looking for spa treatments can find options in the nearby area of Oslo.

Fitness: The hostel does not feature a fitness center. For exercise, guests can use local gyms or enjoy outdoor activities in the city.

Bars

Bar: The hostel does not have a bar on-site. Guests can explore local bars and cafes in the vicinity for drinks and socializing.

Events and Conferences

Meeting Facilities: Anker Hostel does not offer dedicated meeting or conference facilities. For business events or meetings, guests would need to utilize nearby venues or conference centers.

Basic Facilities and Amenities

Rooms: The hostel provides a variety of room options, including:

Dormitories: Shared dormitory-style rooms with bunk beds.

Private Rooms: Basic private rooms with single or double beds.

Bedding: Linens are provided for all rooms.

Technology: Free Wi-Fi available throughout the hostel; some rooms may have TVs.

Bathrooms: Shared or private bathrooms depending on the room type, with modern fixtures and essential toiletries.

Common Areas: Includes communal areas where guests can relax, socialize, and meet fellow travelers.

Kitchen: A shared kitchen is available for guests to prepare their own meals.

Luggage Storage: Luggage storage facilities are provided for guests arriving before check-in or departing after check-out.

Opening and Closing Hours

Reception: Typically open during standard hours, but it's best to confirm specific times with the hostel directly. Some hostels operate with 24-hour reception.

Kitchen: Usually available throughout the day; exact hours may vary.

Price

Rates: Prices at Anker Hostel generally range from €30 to €70 per night, depending on the room type, season, and availability. These rates are competitive for budget accommodations in Oslo.

Pros

Affordable: Provides economical lodging options with essential amenities.

Central Location: Conveniently located near key attractions and public transportation.

Clean and Functional: Offers straightforward and well-maintained facilities.

Shared Facilities: Includes a communal kitchen and common areas for guest use.

Cons

Limited Amenities: Lacks additional amenities such as an on-site bar or fitness center.

Basic Accommodations: Rooms and facilities are functional but minimalistic, with limited personal touches.

Local Tips

Explore the City: Use the hostel's central location to visit nearby attractions such as Karl Johans Gate, the Royal Palace, and the Oslo Opera House.

Public Transport: Utilize nearby tram and bus stops for easy travel around Oslo and to reach other parts of the city.

Local Dining: Check out local cafes and restaurants in the area for affordable and diverse dining options.

2. **Oslo Hostel Central**

Oslo Hostel Central offers economical lodging with a focus on basic comfort and convenience. It provides a straightforward, no-frills experience, making it ideal for budget-conscious travelers who need a central location to explore Oslo.

Location

Address: Bislettgata 4A, 0166 Oslo, Norway

Proximity:

Oslo Central Station: Approximately 15 minutes by foot or a short tram ride.

Karl Johans Gate: About 15 minutes by foot.

The Royal Palace: Around 20 minutes by foot.

Aker Brygge: Approximately 25 minutes by foot or a short tram ride.

Highlights

Budget-Friendly: Provides affordable rates for travelers on a budget.

Central Location: Positioned conveniently near major attractions and public transportation.

Basic Comfort: Offers simple and clean accommodations without extra amenities.

Spa and Wellness

Spa: Oslo Hostel Central does not have an on-site spa. For relaxation and treatments, guests can explore nearby wellness centers in Oslo.

Fitness: The hostel does not feature a fitness center. Local gyms or outdoor spaces are available for exercise.

Bars

Bar: The hostel does not have an on-site bar. Guests can find nearby bars and cafes for drinks and social activities.

Events and Conferences

Meeting Facilities: Oslo Hostel Central does not offer dedicated meeting or conference facilities. For business events, guests will need to use nearby venues or conference centers.

Basic Facilities and Amenities

Rooms: The hostel provides a range of room types, including:

Dormitories: Shared rooms with bunk beds for budget travelers.

Private Rooms: Simple private rooms with single or double beds.

Bedding: Linens are provided in all rooms.

Technology: Free Wi-Fi is available throughout the hostel; some rooms may have TVs.

Bathrooms: Private or shared bathrooms depending on the room type, with modern fixtures and essential toiletries.

Common Areas: Includes communal areas for relaxation and socializing.

Kitchen: A shared kitchen is available for guests to prepare their own meals.

Luggage Storage: Facilities for storing luggage are available for guests arriving before check-in or departing after check-out.

Opening and Closing Hours

Reception: Typically open during standard hours, but specific times may vary. It's best to confirm the hours with the hostel directly.

Kitchen: Usually available throughout the day; exact hours may vary.

Price

Rates: Prices at Oslo Hostel Central generally range from €30 to €60 per night, depending on the room type, season, and availability. These rates are competitive for budget accommodations in Oslo.

Pros

Affordable: Provides budget-friendly rates suitable for cost-conscious travelers.

Central Location: Conveniently located near major attractions and public transport.

Basic and Clean: Offers simple, clean accommodations with essential amenities.

Shared Facilities: Includes a communal kitchen and common areas for guest use.

Cons

Limited Amenities: Lacks additional amenities such as an on-site bar, spa, or fitness center.

Basic Accommodations: Rooms and facilities are functional but minimalistic.

Local Tips

Explore the City: Take advantage of the hostel's central location to visit nearby attractions such as Karl Johans Gate, the Royal Palace, and the Oslo Opera House.

Public Transport: Utilize nearby tram and bus stops for easy travel around Oslo and to explore other parts of the city.

Local Dining: Discover local cafes and restaurants in the vicinity for diverse and affordable dining options.

3. HI Oslo Haraldsheim

HI Oslo Haraldsheim is part of the Hostelling International network and provides affordable, comfortable accommodations in a welcoming environment. The hostel emphasizes a community feel and offers a range of facilities to cater to various types of travelers.

Location

Address: Haraldsheimveien 4, 0894 Oslo, Norway

Proximity:

Oslo Central Station: About 15 minutes by bus or tram.

Karl Johans Gate: Approximately 20 minutes by tram.

The Royal Palace: Around 25 minutes by tram or bus.

Aker Brygge: Approximately 30 minutes by tram or bus.

Highlights

Budget-Friendly: Offers competitive rates for travelers looking for economical accommodations.

Community Atmosphere: Fosters a friendly environment, ideal for meeting fellow travelers.

Modern Facilities: Features contemporary amenities and well-maintained facilities.

Spa and Wellness

Spa: HI Oslo Haraldsheim does not have an on-site spa. For relaxation and treatments, guests can explore local wellness centers in Oslo.

Fitness: The hostel does not offer a fitness center. Nearby gyms or outdoor areas are available for exercise.

Bars

Bar: The hostel does not have a bar. Guests can explore local bars and cafes in the area for drinks and socializing.

Events and Conferences

Meeting Facilities: HI Oslo Haraldsheim does not provide dedicated meeting or conference rooms. For business meetings or events, guests would need to use nearby venues or conference centers.

Basic Facilities and Amenities

Rooms: The hostel offers a variety of room types, including:

Dormitories: Shared dormitory-style rooms with bunk beds.

Private Rooms: Basic private rooms with single or double beds.

Bedding: Linens are provided in all rooms.

Technology: Free Wi-Fi available throughout the hostel; some rooms may have TVs.

Bathrooms: Shared or private bathrooms depending on the room type, with modern fixtures and essential toiletries.

Common Areas: Includes communal areas where guests can relax, socialize, and meet other travelers.

Kitchen: A shared kitchen is available for guests to prepare their own meals.

Luggage Storage: Facilities for storing luggage are available before check-in or after check-out.

Opening and Closing Hours

Reception: Generally open during standard hours, but it's best to check specific times directly with the hostel.

Kitchen: Usually accessible throughout the day; exact hours may vary.

Price

Rates: Prices at HI Oslo Haraldsheim typically range from €40 to €80 per night, depending on the room type, season, and availability. Rates are competitive for budget accommodations in Oslo.

Pros

Affordable: Provides economical lodging options with good value for money.

Community Feel: Offers a friendly atmosphere ideal for meeting other travelers.

Clean and Modern: Features contemporary design and well-maintained facilities.

Shared Facilities: Includes a communal kitchen and common areas for guest use.

Cons

Limited Amenities: Lacks additional amenities such as an on-site bar, spa, or fitness center.

Basic Accommodations: Rooms and facilities are functional but minimalistic.

Local Tips

Explore the Area: Use the hostel's location to visit nearby attractions and utilize public transport to explore further parts of Oslo.

Public Transport: Utilize the nearby tram and bus stops for convenient travel around Oslo.

Local Dining: Check out local cafes and restaurants in the area for affordable and diverse dining options.

4. Cochs Pensjonat

Cochs Pensjonat provides a cozy and budget-friendly stay in Oslo, combining traditional charm with modern amenities. It caters to travelers seeking a more personal and relaxed lodging experience without the higher price tag of luxury hotels.

Location

Address: Bislettgata 8, 0169 Oslo, Norway

Proximity:

Oslo Central Station: About 15 minutes by foot or a short tram ride.

Karl Johans Gate: Approximately 15 minutes by foot.

The Royal Palace: Around 20 minutes by foot.

Aker Brygge: Approximately 25 minutes by foot or a short tram ride.

Highlights

Affordable Rates: Offers budget-friendly pricing that provides good value for money.

Charming Atmosphere: Combines traditional guesthouse warmth with modern amenities.

Central Location: Conveniently located close to major attractions and public transportation.

Spa and Wellness

Spa: Cochs Pensjonat does not have an on-site spa. For relaxation and spa treatments, guests can explore local wellness centers in Oslo.

Fitness: The guesthouse does not offer a fitness center. Nearby gyms or outdoor spaces can be used for exercise.

Bars

Bar: The guesthouse does not have an on-site bar. Guests can find nearby bars and cafes for drinks and socializing.

Events and Conferences

Meeting Facilities: Cochs Pensjonat does not provide dedicated meeting or conference rooms. For business events or meetings, nearby venues or conference centers would be suitable.

Basic Facilities and Amenities

Rooms: The guesthouse offers various room types, including:

Single and Double Rooms: Simple yet comfortable rooms with essential furnishings.

Bedding: High-quality beds and linens for a restful stay.

Technology: Free Wi-Fi and flat-screen TVs.

Bathrooms: Private bathrooms with modern fixtures and complimentary toiletries.

Common Areas: Includes a lounge area where guests can relax and socialize.

Breakfast: A buffet breakfast is typically available, offering a variety of options to start the day.

Concierge Service: The staff can assist with local recommendations, reservations, and other guest needs.

Opening and Closing Hours

Reception: Usually open during standard hours. It is best to confirm specific times directly with the guesthouse.

Breakfast: Served in the morning, generally extending from early to mid-morning.

Common Areas: Accessible throughout the day.

Price

Rates: Prices at Cochs Pensjonat generally range from €60 to €120 per night, depending on the room type, season, and availability. These rates are competitive for budget accommodations in Oslo.

Pros

Affordable: Provides budget-friendly pricing with comfortable and clean accommodations.

Central Location: Conveniently situated near major attractions and public transport.

Charming and Personal: Offers a more intimate and personal lodging experience compared to larger hotels.

Breakfast Included: Buffet breakfast adds value to the stay.

Cons

Limited Amenities: Lacks on-site facilities such as a bar or spa.

Basic Accommodations: Rooms and services are functional but minimalistic.

Local Tips

Explore Nearby: Take advantage of the guesthouse's central location to visit nearby attractions like Karl Johans Gate, the Royal Palace, and the Oslo Opera House.

Public Transport: Use nearby tram and bus stops for convenient travel around Oslo and to explore other parts of the city.

Local Dining: Discover local cafes and restaurants in the area for a variety of dining options.

5. Saga Poshtel Oslo Central

Saga Poshtel Oslo Central is designed to provide affordable, high-quality accommodation with a focus on modern amenities and a welcoming atmosphere. It caters to travelers who seek both comfort and value in the heart of Oslo.

Location

Address: Bislettgata 4, 0164 Oslo, Norway

Proximity:

Oslo Central Station: Approximately 15 minutes by foot or a short tram ride.

Karl Johans Gate: About 10 minutes by foot.

The Royal Palace: Roughly 20 minutes by foot.

Aker Brygge: Around 25 minutes by foot or a short tram ride.

Highlights

Modern Design: Features contemporary design with stylish decor and modern amenities.

Affordable Rates: Offers competitive pricing for budget travelers looking for quality accommodations.

Central Location: Conveniently situated close to Oslo's main attractions and public transportation.

Spa and Wellness

Spa: Saga Poshtel does not have an on-site spa. For relaxation and treatments, guests can explore nearby wellness centers in Oslo.

Fitness: The hostel does not have a fitness center. Nearby gyms or outdoor spaces can be used for exercise.

Bars

Bar: The hostel does not have an on-site bar. However, guests can explore local bars and cafes in the vicinity for drinks and social activities.

Events and Conferences

Meeting Facilities: Saga Poshtel Oslo Central does not offer dedicated meeting or conference rooms. For business events or meetings, guests would need to use nearby venues or conference centers.

Basic Facilities and Amenities

Rooms: The hostel offers a range of room options, including:

Dormitories: Shared dormitory-style rooms with bunk beds.

Private Rooms: Simple private rooms with single or double beds.

Bedding: Linens and comfortable beds are provided.

Technology: Free Wi-Fi available throughout the hostel; some rooms may have flat-screen TVs.

Bathrooms: Private or shared bathrooms depending on the room type, equipped with modern fixtures and essential toiletries.

Common Areas: Includes communal spaces where guests can relax and socialize, including a lounge area.

Kitchen: A shared kitchen is available for guests to prepare their own meals.

Luggage Storage: Facilities for storing luggage are available before check-in or after check-out.

Opening and Closing Hours

Reception: Typically open during standard hours. It's advisable to check specific times directly with the hostel.

Kitchen: Generally accessible throughout the day; specific hours may vary.

Price

Rates: Prices at Saga Poshtel Oslo Central usually range from €40 to €80 per night, depending on the room type, season, and availability. Rates are competitive for budget accommodations in Oslo.

Pros

Modern and Clean: Offers contemporary, clean, and well-maintained facilities.

Affordable: Provides economical lodging options with good value for money.

Central Location: Conveniently located near major attractions and public transport.

Shared Facilities: Includes a communal kitchen and common areas for guest use.

Cons

Limited Amenities: Lacks additional features such as an on-site bar or spa.

Basic Accommodations: Rooms and services are functional but minimalist, focusing on essential needs.

Local Tips

Explore Nearby: Use the hostel's central location to visit attractions like Karl Johans Gate, the Royal Palace, and the Oslo Opera House.

Public Transport: Take advantage of nearby tram and bus stops for easy travel around Oslo and to explore other parts of the city.

Local Dining: Discover local cafes and restaurants in the area for a range of affordable dining options.

Vacation Rentals

Vacation rentals in Oslo offer a home-like experience with the flexibility and comfort of fully equipped apartments or houses. Ideal for longer stays or groups, these rentals provide private living spaces, kitchens, and often unique local charm. Enjoy the convenience and personal touch of a vacation rental while exploring Oslo.

Top 5 Vacation Rentals

1. **The Oslo Suites**

The Oslo Suites provides high-end vacation rentals designed to offer the comfort and privacy of a home with the amenities and services of a hotel. These suites cater to travelers looking for luxurious and spacious accommodations in the heart of Oslo, ideal for both short and extended stays.

Location

Address: The exact address of The Oslo Suites is typically provided upon booking for privacy reasons.

Proximity:

Oslo Central Station: About 10-15 minutes by foot or a short tram ride.

Karl Johans Gate: Approximately 10 minutes by foot.

The Royal Palace: Around 15 minutes by foot.

Aker Brygge: Roughly 20 minutes by foot or a short tram ride.

Highlights

Luxury Accommodations: Offers spacious, well-appointed suites with high-end furnishings and modern decor.

Central Location: Situated close to major attractions, dining, and shopping areas.

Home-Like Comfort: Provides a more personal and private stay compared to traditional hotels.

Spa and Wellness

Spa: The Oslo Suites may not have an on-site spa. Guests can access nearby wellness centers and spas for relaxation and treatments.

Fitness: Suites may not include fitness facilities, but there are local gyms and outdoor spaces available for exercise.

Bars

Bar: The suites typically do not have an on-site bar. Guests can explore a variety of local bars and cafes within walking distance for drinks and socializing.

Events and Conferences

Meeting Facilities: The Oslo Suites generally do not offer dedicated meeting or conference rooms. For business meetings or events, nearby venues or conference centers can be used.

Basic Facilities and Amenities

Suites: The accommodations include various suite types, all designed for comfort and luxury:

Living Area: Spacious living rooms with comfortable seating, flat-screen TVs, and often, modern entertainment systems.

Kitchen: Fully equipped kitchens with high-end appliances, utensils, and dining areas for self-catering.

Bedrooms: Comfortable bedrooms with premium bedding, wardrobes, and sometimes, workspaces.

Bathrooms: Luxurious bathrooms with modern fixtures, complimentary toiletries, and often, in-suite laundry facilities.

Technology: Free high-speed Wi-Fi throughout the suites.

Housekeeping: Regular cleaning services to ensure a comfortable stay.

Concierge Service: Assistance with bookings, recommendations, and other guest needs.

Opening and Closing Hours

Check-In/Check-Out: Standard check-in times are typically in the afternoon, around 3:00 PM, and check-out times are in the morning, around 11:00 AM. Early check-in and late check-out may be available upon request.

Price

Rates: Prices at The Oslo Suites typically range from €150 to €400 per night, depending on the suite type, season, and availability. These rates reflect the premium nature of the accommodations.

Pros

Luxury and Comfort: Provides high-end accommodations with spacious and well-appointed suites.

Central Location: Conveniently located near major attractions, dining, and shopping areas.

Home-Like Feel: Offers a private and personal stay with the comfort of a home.

Fully Equipped: Includes all necessary amenities for a comfortable stay, from kitchens to entertainment systems.

Cons

No On-Site Spa or Fitness Center: Lacks in-house wellness and fitness facilities.

No On-Site Bar: Does not have a bar, requiring guests to visit nearby establishments for drinks.

Higher Price Point: Rates are higher compared to budget accommodations, reflecting the luxury nature of the suites.

Local Tips

Explore the Neighborhood: Take advantage of the central location to explore nearby attractions like Karl Johans Gate, the Royal Palace, and Aker Brygge.

Public Transport: Use the nearby tram and bus stops for convenient travel around Oslo and to other parts of the city.

Local Dining: Discover a variety of local cafes, restaurants, and bars in the area for diverse and high-quality dining options.

Grocery Shopping: Utilize the fully equipped kitchen by shopping at local grocery stores and markets to prepare meals in the suite.

2. Frogner House Apartments – Skovveien 8

Frogner House Apartments – Skovveien 8 offers fully furnished apartments designed to provide guests with a comfortable and luxurious living experience. The apartments feature modern amenities and stylish interiors, catering to business travelers, families, and tourists looking for a high-end accommodation option in Oslo.

Location

Address: Skovveien 8, 0257 Oslo, Norway

Proximity:

Oslo Central Station: Approximately 10-15 minutes by tram or a 25-minute walk.

Karl Johans Gate: About 20 minutes by foot or a short tram ride.

The Royal Palace: Around 10 minutes by foot.

Aker Brygge: Roughly 15 minutes by foot or a short tram ride.

Frogner Park: A 10-minute walk.

Highlights

Luxurious Living: Fully furnished and stylish apartments with modern amenities.

Convenient Location: Situated in a prestigious neighborhood, close to major attractions, dining, and shopping.

Home-Like Comfort: Provides the comfort and convenience of a home with the services of a hotel.

Spa and Wellness

Spa: Frogner House Apartments – Skovveien 8 does not have an on-site spa. Guests can visit nearby wellness centers and spas for relaxation and treatments.

Fitness: The apartment complex does not feature a fitness center. However, there are local gyms and outdoor spaces, such as Frogner Park, available for exercise.

Bars

Bar: There is no on-site bar. Guests can explore a variety of local bars, cafes, and restaurants in the Frogner neighborhood for drinks and socializing.

Events and Conferences

Meeting Facilities: Frogner House Apartments – Skovveien 8 does not offer dedicated meeting or conference rooms. For business events or meetings, guests can use nearby venues or conference centers.

Basic Facilities and Amenities

Apartments: The property offers a range of apartment types, including:

Studios: Compact units with a combined living and sleeping area, kitchenette, and private bathroom.

One-Bedroom Apartments: Separate bedroom, living area, fully equipped kitchen, and private bathroom.

Two-Bedroom Apartments: Ideal for families or groups, featuring multiple bedrooms, a spacious living area, a fully equipped kitchen, and private bathrooms.

Bedding: High-quality beds and linens for a comfortable stay.

Technology: Free high-speed Wi-Fi, flat-screen TVs, and modern entertainment systems.

Bathrooms: Modern bathrooms with essential toiletries and often include in-unit laundry facilities.

Kitchen: Fully equipped kitchens with high-end appliances, utensils, and dining areas for self-catering.

Housekeeping: Regular cleaning services are provided to maintain the apartments.

Concierge Service: Assistance with bookings, recommendations, and other guest needs.

Opening and Closing Hours

Check-In/Check-Out: Standard check-in times are typically in the afternoon, around 3:00 PM, and check-out times are in the morning, around 11:00 AM. Early check-in and late check-out may be available upon request.

Price

Rates: Prices at Frogner House Apartments – Skovveien 8 generally range from €100 to €300 per night, depending on the apartment type, season, and availability. These rates reflect the premium nature of the accommodations.

Pros

Luxury and Comfort: Provides high-end, spacious, and well-furnished apartments.

Central Location: Situated in a prestigious neighborhood close to major attractions, dining, and shopping.

Home-Like Feel: Offers a more private and comfortable stay compared to traditional hotels.

Fully Equipped: Includes all necessary amenities for a comfortable stay, from kitchens to entertainment systems.

Cons

No On-Site Spa or Fitness Center: Lacks in-house wellness and fitness facilities.

No On-Site Bar: Does not have a bar, requiring guests to visit nearby establishments for drinks.

Higher Price Point: Rates are higher compared to budget accommodations, reflecting the luxury nature of the apartments.

Local Tips

Explore the Neighborhood: Take advantage of the central location to visit nearby attractions like the Royal Palace, Karl Johans Gate, and Aker Brygge.

Public Transport: Utilize nearby tram and bus stops for convenient travel around Oslo and to explore other parts of the city.

Local Dining: Discover a variety of local cafes, restaurants, and bars in the Frogner area for diverse and high-quality dining options.

Visit Frogner Park: Just a short walk away, Frogner Park is perfect for a leisurely stroll and is home to the famous Vigeland Sculpture Park.

3. Norwegian Apartments – Bislett

Norwegian Apartments – Bislett offers contemporary and well-furnished apartments designed to provide a comfortable and convenient stay. These apartments cater to both short-term and long-term visitors, making them ideal for tourists, business travelers, and families.

Location

Address: Typically situated in the Bislett neighborhood, the exact address is provided upon booking.

Proximity:

Oslo Central Station: Approximately 20 minutes by foot or a short tram ride.

Karl Johans Gate: Around 15 minutes by foot.

The Royal Palace: About 15 minutes by foot.

Bislett Stadium: Just a few minutes by foot.

Majorstuen: A popular shopping and dining district, roughly 10-15 minutes by foot.

Highlights

Modern Amenities: Fully furnished apartments with contemporary decor and modern conveniences.

Convenient Location: Centrally located with easy access to major attractions, public transportation, and dining options.

Flexible Stays: Suitable for both short-term and extended stays.

Spa and Wellness

Spa: Norwegian Apartments – Bislett does not have an on-site spa. Guests can visit nearby wellness centers and spas in Oslo for relaxation and treatments.

Fitness: The apartments do not have a fitness center, but there are local gyms and outdoor spaces, such as Frogner Park, available for exercise.

Bars

Bar: There is no on-site bar at Norwegian Apartments – Bislett. However, the Bislett neighborhood and nearby Majorstuen offer a variety of bars, cafes, and restaurants for drinks and socializing.

Events and Conferences

Meeting Facilities: The apartments do not offer dedicated meeting or conference rooms. For business events or meetings, nearby venues or conference centers can be used.

Basic Facilities and Amenities

Apartments: The property offers a range of apartment types, including:

Studios: Compact units with a combined living and sleeping area, kitchenette, and private bathroom.

One-Bedroom Apartments: Separate bedroom, living area, fully equipped kitchen, and private bathroom.

Two-Bedroom Apartments: Ideal for families or groups, featuring multiple bedrooms, a spacious living area, a fully equipped kitchen, and private bathrooms.

Bedding: High-quality beds and linens for a comfortable stay.

Technology: Free high-speed Wi-Fi, flat-screen TVs, and modern entertainment systems.

Bathrooms: Modern bathrooms with essential toiletries and often include in-unit laundry facilities.

Kitchen: Fully equipped kitchens with high-end appliances, utensils, and dining areas for self-catering.

Housekeeping: Regular cleaning services are provided to maintain the apartments.

Concierge Service: Assistance with bookings, recommendations, and other guest needs.

Opening and Closing Hours

Check-In/Check-Out: Standard check-in times are typically in the afternoon, around 3:00 PM, and check-out times are in the morning, around 11:00 AM. Early check-in and late check-out may be available upon request.

Price

Rates: Prices at Norwegian Apartments – Bislett generally range from €80 to €200 per night, depending on the apartment type, season, and availability. These rates reflect the mid-range to high-end nature of the accommodations.

Pros

Modern and Comfortable: Provides well-furnished, contemporary apartments with all necessary amenities.

Central Location: Situated in a convenient neighborhood with easy access to major attractions, public transportation, and dining options.

Flexible Stays: Suitable for both short-term and extended stays.

Fully Equipped: Includes all necessary amenities for a comfortable stay, from kitchens to entertainment systems.

Cons

No On-Site Spa or Fitness Center: Lacks in-house wellness and fitness facilities.

No On-Site Bar: Does not have a bar, requiring guests to visit nearby establishments for drinks.

Higher Price Point: Rates are higher compared to budget accommodations, reflecting the quality of the apartments.

Local Tips

Explore the Neighborhood: Take advantage of the central location to visit nearby attractions like the Royal Palace, Karl Johans Gate, and Majorstuen.

Public Transport: Utilize nearby tram and bus stops for convenient travel around Oslo and to explore other parts of the city.

Local Dining: Discover a variety of local cafes, restaurants, and bars in the Bislett area for diverse and high-quality dining options.

Visit Bislett Stadium: Check out local sports events or enjoy a run at the historic Bislett Stadium.

4. **The Hub Apartments**

The Hub Apartments provides a high-end living experience with fully furnished apartments equipped with modern amenities. These apartments cater to both short-term and long-term visitors, making them ideal for tourists, business travelers, and families who want a luxurious home base in the heart of Oslo.

Location

Address: The exact address of The Hub Apartments is typically provided upon booking for privacy reasons.

Proximity:

Oslo Central Station: Approximately 5-10 minutes by foot.

Karl Johans Gate: Around 5 minutes by foot.

The Royal Palace: About 15 minutes by foot.

Aker Brygge: Roughly 20 minutes by foot or a short tram ride.

Opera House: About 10 minutes by foot.

Highlights

Luxury Accommodations: Offers spacious, well-appointed apartments with high-end furnishings and modern decor.

Central Location: Situated close to major attractions, dining, and shopping areas.

Home-Like Comfort: Provides the comfort and convenience of a home with the services of a hotel.

Spa and Wellness

Spa: The Hub Apartments does not have an on-site spa. Guests can access nearby wellness centers and spas for relaxation and treatments.

Fitness: The apartment complex does not feature a fitness center. However, there are local gyms and outdoor spaces available for exercise.

Bars

Bar: There is no on-site bar at The Hub Apartments. Guests can explore a variety of local bars, cafes, and restaurants within walking distance for drinks and social activities.

Events and Conferences

Meeting Facilities: The Hub Apartments generally do not offer dedicated meeting or conference rooms. For business events or meetings, nearby venues or conference centers can be used.

Basic Facilities and Amenities

Apartments: The property offers a range of apartment types, including:

Studios: Compact units with a combined living and sleeping area, kitchenette, and private bathroom.

One-Bedroom Apartments: Separate bedroom, living area, fully equipped kitchen, and private bathroom.

Two-Bedroom Apartments: Ideal for families or groups, featuring multiple bedrooms, a spacious living area, a fully equipped kitchen, and private bathrooms.

Bedding: High-quality beds and linens for a comfortable stay.

Technology: Free high-speed Wi-Fi, flat-screen TVs, and modern entertainment systems.

Bathrooms: Modern bathrooms with essential toiletries and often include in-unit laundry facilities.

Kitchen: Fully equipped kitchens with high-end appliances, utensils, and dining areas for self-catering.

Housekeeping: Regular cleaning services are provided to maintain the apartments.

Concierge Service: Assistance with bookings, recommendations, and other guest needs.

Opening and Closing Hours

Check-In/Check-Out: Standard check-in times are typically in the afternoon, around 3:00 PM, and check-out times are in the morning, around 11:00 AM. Early check-in and late check-out may be available upon request.

Price

Rates: Prices at The Hub Apartments typically range from €150 to €400 per night, depending on the apartment type, season, and availability. These rates reflect the premium nature of the accommodations.

Pros

Luxury and Comfort: Provides high-end, spacious, and well-furnished apartments.

Central Location: Situated in a convenient neighborhood close to major attractions, dining, and shopping areas.

Home-Like Feel: Offers a more private and comfortable stay compared to traditional hotels.

Fully Equipped: Includes all necessary amenities for a comfortable stay, from kitchens to entertainment systems.

Cons

No On-Site Spa or Fitness Center: Lacks in-house wellness and fitness facilities.

No On-Site Bar: Does not have a bar, requiring guests to visit nearby establishments for drinks.

Higher Price Point: Rates are higher compared to budget accommodations, reflecting the luxury nature of the apartments.

Local Tips

Explore the Neighborhood: Take advantage of the central location to visit nearby attractions like Karl Johans Gate, the Royal Palace, and Aker Brygge.

Public Transport: Utilize nearby tram and bus stops for convenient travel around Oslo and to explore other parts of the city.

Local Dining: Discover a variety of local cafes, restaurants, and bars in the area for diverse and high-quality dining options.

Visit the Opera House: Just a short walk away, the Oslo Opera House offers stunning architecture and a range of performances.

5. Vika Apartments

Vika Apartments offers a range of serviced apartments designed to provide a home-like atmosphere with the amenities of a hotel. They cater to both short-term and long-term stays, making them ideal for tourists, business travelers, and families who want the convenience of a central location with the comfort of a private apartment.

Location

Address: The exact address is typically provided upon booking, but Vika Apartments is located in the Vika neighborhood.

Proximity:

Oslo Central Station: About 15-20 minutes by foot or a short tram ride.

Karl Johans Gate: Around 10-15 minutes by foot.

The Royal Palace: Approximately 10 minutes by foot.

Aker Brygge: Just 5-10 minutes by foot.

Vigeland Park: About 20 minutes by foot or a short tram ride.

Highlights

Modern Living: Offers contemporary, well-furnished apartments with high-end amenities.

Prime Location: Situated in one of Oslo's most desirable neighborhoods, close to major attractions, shopping, and dining.

Flexibility: Ideal for both short-term and long-term stays.

Spa and Wellness

Spa: Vika Apartments does not have an on-site spa, but there are several nearby wellness centers and spas for relaxation and treatments.

Fitness: The apartments do not feature a fitness center, but there are local gyms and outdoor spaces available for exercise.

Bars

Bar: There is no on-site bar at Vika Apartments, but the neighborhood is home to numerous bars, cafes, and restaurants where guests can enjoy a drink.

Events and Conferences

Meeting Facilities: Vika Apartments does not offer dedicated meeting or conference rooms. For business events or meetings, guests can use nearby venues or conference centers.

Basic Facilities and Amenities

Apartments: The property offers a variety of apartment types, including:

Studios: Compact units with a combined living and sleeping area, kitchenette, and private bathroom.

One-Bedroom Apartments: Separate bedroom, living area, fully equipped kitchen, and private bathroom.

Two-Bedroom Apartments: Ideal for families or groups, featuring multiple bedrooms, a spacious living area, a fully equipped kitchen, and private bathrooms.

Bedding: High-quality beds and linens for a comfortable stay.

Technology: Free high-speed Wi-Fi, flat-screen TVs, and modern entertainment systems.

Bathrooms: Modern bathrooms with essential toiletries and often include in-unit laundry facilities.

Kitchen: Fully equipped kitchens with high-end appliances, utensils, and dining areas for self-catering.

Housekeeping: Regular cleaning services are provided to maintain the apartments.

Concierge Service: Assistance with bookings, recommendations, and other guest needs.

Opening and Closing Hours

Check-In/Check-Out: Standard check-in times are typically in the afternoon, around 3:00 PM, and check-out times are in the morning, around 11:00 AM. Early check-in and late check-out may be available upon request.

Price

Rates: Prices at Vika Apartments typically range from €100 to €300 per night, depending on the apartment type, season, and availability. These rates reflect the high-end nature of the accommodations.

Pros

Modern and Comfortable: Provides well-furnished, contemporary apartments with all necessary amenities.

Prime Location: Situated in a prestigious neighborhood close to major attractions, dining, and shopping.

Flexibility: Suitable for both short-term and extended stays.

Fully Equipped: Includes all necessary amenities for a comfortable stay, from kitchens to entertainment systems.

Cons

No On-Site Spa or Fitness Center: Lacks in-house wellness and fitness facilities.

No On-Site Bar: Does not have a bar, requiring guests to visit nearby establishments for drinks.

Higher Price Point: Rates are higher compared to budget accommodations, reflecting the quality of the apartments.

Local Tips

Explore the Neighborhood: Take advantage of the central location to visit nearby attractions like Aker Brygge, the Royal Palace, and Karl Johans Gate.

Public Transport: Utilize nearby tram and bus stops for convenient travel around Oslo and to explore other parts of the city.

Local Dining: Discover a variety of local cafes, restaurants, and bars in the Vika area for diverse and high-quality dining options.

Visit Vigeland Park: Just a short tram ride away, the park offers beautiful sculptures and green spaces for relaxation.

Chapter 8: Cultural Experiences

Festivals and Events

Oslo is a vibrant city with a rich cultural scene, offering a wide array of festivals and events throughout the year. These cultural experiences provide tourists with a unique opportunity to engage with the local culture, arts, and traditions. Here's an extensive overview of the major festivals and events in Oslo that you should consider during your visit:

Festivals and Events in Oslo

1. Oslo Jazz Festival

Overview: One of Oslo's premier music festivals, the Oslo Jazz Festival, celebrates jazz in all its forms. The event attracts both international jazz stars and local talent, featuring performances in various venues around the city.

When: Typically held in August.

Highlights: Diverse jazz performances, workshops, and jam sessions. Venues include clubs, concert halls, and open-air spaces.

Location: Various locations around Oslo, including the Oslo Concert Hall and smaller jazz clubs.

2. Oslo International Film Festival

Overview: This festival showcases a selection of international and Norwegian films, providing a platform for filmmakers and offering film enthusiasts a chance to see a variety of genres and styles.

When: Usually held in October.

Highlights: Film screenings, director Q&As, and workshops. The festival often includes both feature films and short films.

Location: Venues include cinemas such as the Cinema Klingenberg and the Oslo Opera House.

3. Øya Festival

Overview: Øya Festival is a major music festival known for its diverse lineup that spans genres from rock and pop to electronic and indie. It's one of Norway's largest and most renowned music festivals.

When: Held annually in August.

Highlights: Live performances by international and local artists, food stalls, and art installations. The festival is known for its eco-friendly initiatives.

Location: Held at Tøyenparken, a large park in Oslo.

4. Norwegian Wood Music Festival

Overview: Norwegian Wood is another prominent music festival that features a mix of international and Norwegian artists, including rock, pop, and alternative music.

When: Typically takes place in June.

Highlights: Concerts by well-known bands and artists, along with local acts.

Location: Held at the Frogner Park, offering a scenic outdoor venue.

5. Oslo Medieval Park (Gamlebyen)

Overview: This is not a festival but an ongoing attraction that brings Oslo's medieval history to life. Visitors can experience reenactments, traditional crafts, and medieval cuisine.

When: Open during the summer months, with special events and activities throughout.

Highlights: Historical reenactments, workshops, and guided tours.

Location: Located in the Old Town area (Gamlebyen).

6. Oslo Pride

Overview: Oslo Pride is the city's annual LGBTQ+ pride festival, celebrating diversity and inclusion with a wide range of events.

When: Typically held in June.

Highlights: Pride parade, parties, cultural events, and discussions on LGBTQ+ rights and issues.

Location: Various locations around Oslo, including a large parade through the city center.

7. Oslo Food Festival

Overview: A celebration of Oslo's culinary scene, featuring local and international food and drink.

When: Usually held in September.

Highlights: Food stalls, cooking demonstrations, and tastings. The festival showcases local produce, gourmet foods, and innovative cuisine.

Location: Held at various locations, including Aker Brygge and Rådhusplassen (City Hall Square).

8. Sami Week (Sámi Veahkki)

Overview: Sami Week celebrates the culture and heritage of the Sami people, the indigenous people of the Arctic region.

When: Held in February.

Highlights: Cultural events, traditional Sami music, crafts, and cuisine. The week often features educational programs about Sami traditions and history.

Location: Various venues in Oslo, including cultural centers and public spaces.

9. Oslo Christmas Market

Overview: The Oslo Christmas Market is a festive event that transforms the city into a winter wonderland with holiday decorations, crafts, and seasonal treats.

When: Held from late November to late December.

Highlights: Holiday stalls, Christmas lights, traditional Norwegian foods, and entertainment.

Location: Traditionally held in areas like Spikersuppa and the city center.

10. Oslo Book Fair (Den Norske Bokhandlerforening)

Overview: The Oslo Book Fair is a major event for book lovers, featuring book launches, author readings, and literary discussions.

When: Usually takes place in September.

Highlights: Book signings, panel discussions, and a wide range of books and literary merchandise.

Location: Oslo Spektrum and other venues.

Local Tips

Check Event Schedules: Festivals and events can vary year to year, so it's a good idea to check the schedule and book tickets in advance if needed.

Public Transport: Utilize Oslo's efficient public transportation system to get to various event locations. Trams, buses, and the metro can help you navigate the city easily.

Dress Accordingly: Depending on the time of year and the type of event, be prepared for weather conditions. For outdoor festivals, dress in layers and bring rain gear if necessary.

Explore Local Cuisine: Many festivals, especially food festivals, offer a chance to sample local Norwegian dishes and international cuisine.

Theatres and Performing Arts

Oslo boasts a vibrant theatre and performing arts scene that caters to a wide range of interests, from classical performances and contemporary theatre to experimental art and dance. Here's an extensive overview of the key theatres and performing arts venues in Oslo:

Theatres and Performing Arts Venues in Oslo

1. Nationaltheatret (The National Theatre)

Overview: Norway's largest and most prestigious theatre, Nationaltheatret offers a diverse program of classic and contemporary plays, including works by Norwegian and international playwrights.

Address: Johanne Dybwads plass 1, 0161 Oslo

Highlights: Renowned for high-quality productions, including Norwegian classics, modern dramas, and international works. The theatre has several stages, including the Main Stage and the Scene West.

Website: nationaltheatret.no

2. Oslo Opera House (Den Norske Opera & Ballett)

Overview: The Oslo Opera House is a stunning architectural landmark and the home of the Norwegian National Opera and Ballet. It hosts a variety of performances, including opera, ballet, and classical music concerts.

Address: Kirsten Flagstads Plass 1, 0150 Oslo

Highlights: The venue itself is an architectural marvel with a sloping roof that visitors can walk on. Performances include opera productions, ballet, and orchestral concerts.

Website: operaen.no

3. Det Norske Teatret (The Norwegian Theatre)

Overview: Known for its emphasis on contemporary theatre, Det Norske Teatret presents a mix of Norwegian and international works, including both drama and comedy.

Address: Kristian IVs gate 8, 0164 Oslo

Highlights: Offers a diverse range of performances, including new plays, adaptations of literature, and contemporary works.

Website: detnorsketeatret.no

4. Oslo Nye Teater

Overview: Oslo Nye Teater is one of Oslo's major theatres, offering a broad repertoire of performances, from classic plays to modern dramas and musicals.

Address: St. Olavs gate 3, 0165 Oslo

Highlights: Known for its wide-ranging program, including popular musicals, dramatic plays, and family-friendly shows.

Website: oslonye.no

5. Black Box Teater

Overview: Black Box Teater is a prominent venue for contemporary and experimental theatre, offering innovative performances and performances by both local and international artists.

Address: Marstrandgata 8, 0170 Oslo

Highlights: Focuses on avant-garde and experimental performances, including dance, theatre, and interdisciplinary works.

Website: blackbox.no

6. Teater Ibsen

Overview: Teater Ibsen is dedicated to the works of Henrik Ibsen, Norway's most famous playwright. It stages Ibsen's plays as well as works inspired by his legacy.

Address: Bislettgata 2, 0178 Oslo

Highlights: Focuses on Ibsen's classic works and their modern interpretations, providing a deep dive into Norwegian theatre history.

Website: teateribsen.no

7. Kulturhuset (The Culture House)

Overview: Kulturhuset is a versatile cultural venue that hosts a variety of performing arts, including theatre, music, and dance. It also serves as a meeting place for cultural and community events.

Address: Youngs gate 6, 0181 Oslo

Highlights: Offers a diverse program that includes both established performances and experimental works.

Website: kulturhuset.no

8. Norsk Teater (Norwegian Theatre)

Overview: Known for its rich history and focus on Norwegian drama, Norsk Teater presents a range of performances from classic plays to modern interpretations.

Address: Bislettgata 4, 0178 Oslo

Highlights: Emphasizes Norwegian playwrights and classic works, often featuring well-known actors and high-quality productions.

Website: norskteater.no

9. Dansens Hus (House of Dance)

Overview: Dansens Hus is a key venue for contemporary dance in Oslo, showcasing performances by Norwegian and international choreographers.

Address: Vulkan 1, 0178 Oslo

Highlights: Offers a range of dance performances, workshops, and residencies, making it a hub for the contemporary dance scene.

Website: dansenshus.com

10. Teaterverkstedet

Overview: A space for experimental and community-driven theatre, Teaterverkstedet focuses on emerging artists and innovative performances.

Address: Øvre Slottsgate 2, 0157 Oslo

Highlights: Provides a platform for new and experimental works, offering a more intimate and interactive theatre experience.

Website: teaterverkstedet.no

Local Tips

Book in Advance: Popular performances can sell out quickly, so it's wise to book tickets in advance.

Check Schedules: Theatres often have varying schedules, so check their websites for the latest information on performances and timings.

Explore Different Genres: Oslo's theatres offer a wide range of genres and styles, so consider exploring different types of performances to get a full taste of the local cultural scene.

Public Transport: Use Oslo's public transport system to easily reach theatres and performing arts venues around the city.

Music and Concerts

Oslo is a dynamic city with a thriving music scene that caters to a wide range of tastes and interests. From classical concerts and opera performances to rock gigs and electronic dance music, Oslo offers a variety of musical experiences. Here's an extensive overview of the key venues and events for music and concerts in Oslo:

Music and Concert Venues in Oslo

1. Oslo Opera House (Den Norske Opera & Ballett)

Overview: This iconic venue is home to the Norwegian National Opera and Ballet and hosts a variety of performances, including opera, ballet, and classical music concerts.

Address: Kirsten Flagstads Plass 1, 0150 Oslo

Highlights: The building itself is an architectural marvel, and its performance schedule includes world-class operas, ballets, and orchestral concerts.

Website: operaen.no

2. Oslo Concert Hall (Oslo Konserthus)

Overview: Oslo Concert Hall is a premier venue for classical music and jazz performances. It's known for its excellent acoustics and hosts a variety of concerts throughout the year.

Address: Fridtjof Nansens Plass 1, 0160 Oslo

Highlights: Home to the Oslo Philharmonic Orchestra, the hall features classical music, jazz, and occasional pop and rock concerts.

Website: konserthuset.no

3. Vulkan Arena

Overview: Vulkan Arena is a versatile venue for live music, hosting concerts ranging from rock and pop to electronic and hip-hop.

Address: Vulkan 1, 0178 Oslo

Highlights: Known for its lively atmosphere and diverse music lineup, Vulkan Arena features both international and local artists.

Website: vulkanarena.no

4. Blå

Overview: Blå is a renowned club and live music venue famous for its eclectic lineup, including jazz, electronic, hip-hop, and indie music.

Address: Brenneriveien 9C, 0182 Oslo

Highlights: Offers an intimate setting with a focus on innovative and experimental music, as well as a vibrant nightlife scene.

Website: blaa.oslo.no

5. Parkteatret

Overview: Parkteatret is a popular venue for concerts and events, featuring a wide range of musical genres from indie rock to electronic.

Address: Olaf Ryes Plass 11, 0552 Oslo

Highlights: The venue has a relaxed atmosphere and hosts both local and international acts.

Website: parkteatret.no

6. Sentrum Scene

Overview: Sentrum Scene is one of Oslo's major concert venues, hosting large-scale concerts and events across various genres.

Address: Arteriusgata 8, 0183 Oslo

Highlights: Features performances by well-known international artists and bands, making it a key venue for major music events.

Website: sentrumscene.no

7. Rockefeller Music Hall

Overview: Rockefeller Music Hall is a prominent venue for rock, metal, and alternative music, as well as other genres like folk and indie.

Address: Badstugata 2, 0183 Oslo

Highlights: Known for its high-energy performances and hosting both established and emerging artists.

Website: rockefeller.no

8. Oslo Spektrum

Overview: Oslo Spektrum is a large indoor arena that hosts major concerts, sports events, and entertainment shows.

Address: Sonja Henies Plass 2, 0185 Oslo

Highlights: Features performances by big-name artists and bands, as well as a variety of other events.

Website: oslospektrum.no

9. Nasjonal Jazzscene

Overview: Nasjonal Jazzscene is a leading venue for jazz performances, showcasing both Norwegian and international jazz talent.

Address: Haugtussa 1, 0177 Oslo

Highlights: Known for its intimate setting and high-quality jazz performances.

Website: jazzscene.no

10. Kulturhuset

Overview: Kulturhuset is a cultural venue that hosts a range of musical performances, including live music, DJ sets, and other events.

Address: Youngs gate 6, 0181 Oslo

Highlights: Offers a diverse program that includes both established and up-and-coming artists.

Website: kulturhuset.no

Major Music Festivals in Oslo

1. Øya Festival

Overview: Øya Festival is one of Norway's largest and most popular music festivals, featuring a wide range of genres including rock, pop, indie, and electronic music.

When: Held annually in August.

Highlights: Includes performances by top international and local artists, as well as food stalls, art installations, and eco-friendly initiatives.

Location: Tøyenparken.

2. Norwegian Wood Music Festival

Overview: Norwegian Wood is a prominent music festival known for its diverse lineup, including rock, pop, and alternative music.

When: Typically held in June.

Highlights: Features performances by both international and Norwegian artists in a picturesque park setting.

Location: Frogner Park.

3. Oslo Jazz Festival

Overview: The Oslo Jazz Festival celebrates jazz music with performances from international jazz stars and local talent.

When: Usually held in August.

Highlights: Offers a range of jazz styles and includes workshops and jam sessions.

Location: Various venues around Oslo.

4. Oslo World Music Festival

Overview: Oslo World Music Festival focuses on global music, bringing together artists from around the world to perform traditional and contemporary music.

When: Held annually in November.

Highlights: Features performances, workshops, and cultural events that showcase diverse musical traditions.

Location: Various venues in Oslo.

Local Tips

Check Schedules: Always check the schedules and availability for concerts and events, as they can sell out quickly.

Explore Different Genres: Oslo's music scene is diverse, so consider exploring different genres and venues to get a full experience.

Public Transport: Utilize Oslo's public transportation system to easily reach different music venues and festivals.

Early Arrival: Arriving early can help you secure good seats or a spot in the front row, especially for popular concerts.

Art Galleries

Oslo is home to a diverse array of art galleries that showcase everything from contemporary art and classic Norwegian works to international masterpieces. Here's an extensive overview of some of the key art galleries in Oslo that are worth visiting:

Art Galleries in Oslo

1. The National Museum (Nasjonalmuseet)

Overview: The National Museum is Norway's largest art institution, housing an extensive collection of art, design, and architecture. It includes works from the Middle Ages to contemporary art.

Address: Universitetsgata 13, 0164 Oslo

Highlights: Features works by Norwegian masters like Edvard Munch and other international artists. The museum also includes decorative arts and design, as well as architecture.

Website: nasjonalmuseet.no

2. Munch Museum (Munchmuseet)

Overview: Dedicated to the works of Edvard Munch, the Munch Museum is a key destination for those interested in one of Norway's most famous artists.

Address: Tøyengata 53, 0578 Oslo

Highlights: Displays a large collection of Munch's paintings, prints, and sketches, including iconic works like "The Scream." The museum also offers temporary exhibitions and educational programs.

Website: munchmuseet.no

3. Astrup Fearnley Museum

Overview: This contemporary art museum is known for its impressive collection of modern and contemporary art, both Norwegian and international.

Address: Strandpromenaden 2, 0252 Oslo

Highlights: Includes works by major contemporary artists, with a focus on innovative and thought-provoking exhibitions. The museum's building, designed by Renzo Piano, is also notable for its architecture.

Website: afmuseet.no

4. Kunstnernes Hus

Overview: Kunstnernes Hus (Artists' House) is a historic venue dedicated to contemporary art and exhibitions by both Norwegian and international artists.

Address: Bislettgata 32, 0166 Oslo

Highlights: Hosts a range of exhibitions, artist talks, and events, with a focus on contemporary visual art. The building itself is an important piece of architectural history.

Website: kunstnerneshus.no

5. Nordenfjeldske Kunstindustrimuseum

Overview: While primarily known as a design museum, it features a significant collection of decorative arts and design, including contemporary works.

Address: Bislettgata 1, 0350 Oslo

Highlights: Includes design objects, furniture, textiles, and ceramics, showcasing the intersection of art and design.

Website: kunstindustrimuseet.no

6. Oslo Kunstforening

Overview: Oslo Kunstforening is a gallery dedicated to contemporary art, with a focus on showcasing emerging and established artists.

Address: Wergelandsveien 17, 0167 Oslo

Highlights: Features rotating exhibitions of contemporary art in various media, including painting, sculpture, and installation.

Website: kunstforeningen.no

7. Galleri Nobel

Overview: Galleri Nobel is known for its exhibitions of modern and contemporary art, featuring both Norwegian and international artists.

Address: Stortingsgata 16, 0161 Oslo

Highlights: Offers a platform for both established and emerging artists, with a focus on contemporary visual art.

Website: gallerinobel.no

8. Ravnedalen Kunstnerhus

Overview: Ravnedalen Kunstnerhus is an artist-run gallery that focuses on contemporary art and experimental exhibitions.

Address: Bislettgata 2, 0177 Oslo

Highlights: Provides a space for innovative and experimental art practices, including installations, video art, and performance.

Website: ravnedalen.no

9. Galleri 21

Overview: A contemporary art gallery known for its diverse exhibitions and focus on both established and emerging artists.

Address: Dronningens gate 21, 0154 Oslo

Highlights: Features exhibitions of contemporary art, including painting, sculpture, and multimedia works.

Website: galleri21.no

10. Oslo Open

Overview: Oslo Open is an annual event that offers a behind-the-scenes look at the studios and workspaces of Oslo's artists. While not a traditional gallery, it provides a unique opportunity to engage with the local art scene.

When: Typically held in April.

Highlights: Studio visits, artist talks, and exhibitions throughout the city.

Website: osloopen.no

Local Tips

Check Opening Hours: Many galleries have varying opening hours, so it's a good idea to check their websites or call ahead.

Explore Different Neighborhoods: Oslo's art galleries are spread across different neighborhoods, so exploring various areas can give you a broader view of the local art scene.

Attend Openings and Events: Gallery openings and special events are great opportunities to meet artists and see new works.

Public Transport: Oslo's efficient public transport system can help you easily navigate between different galleries and art spaces.

Historical Sites

Oslo is a city rich in history, offering a range of historical sites that reflect its past, from medieval times to modern history. Here's an extensive guide to some of the most significant historical sites in Oslo:

Historical Sites in Oslo

1. Akershus Fortress (Akershus Festning)

Overview: Akershus Fortress is a medieval castle that has served as a royal residence, military stronghold, and government center. It is a key historical site and offers insight into Norway's medieval and modern history.

Address: Akershus festning, 0150 Oslo

Highlights: Explore the well-preserved medieval architecture, enjoy panoramic views of the Oslo Fjord, and visit the Norwegian Resistance Museum and the Armed Forces Museum located within the fortress.

Website: forsvarsbygg.no

2. Oslo City Hall (Rådhuset)

Overview: Oslo City Hall is an iconic building known for its distinctive architecture and role as the venue for the Nobel Peace Prize ceremony. It's a significant landmark in Oslo's political and cultural history.

Address: Rådhusplassen 1, 0037 Oslo

Highlights: The building features intricate murals depicting Norwegian history and culture. Guided tours are available, offering insights into the building's history and artistic decorations.

Website: byrum.oslo.kommune.no

3. The Viking Ship Museum (Vikingskipshuset)

Overview: The Viking Ship Museum houses some of the best-preserved Viking ships and artifacts, providing a fascinating glimpse into Viking history and culture.

Address: Huk Aveny 35, 0287 Oslo

Highlights: View the Oseberg, Gokstad, and Tune ships, along with a range of Viking artifacts such as burial items and household objects. Note that the museum is set to move to the new Museum of the Viking Age on Bygdøy in the near future.

Website: kulturhistorisk.museum.no

4. Nobel Peace Center

Overview: The Nobel Peace Center is dedicated to the Nobel Peace Prize and its laureates, offering exhibitions and educational programs on peace and conflict resolution.

Address: Brynjulf Bulls Plass 1, 0250 Oslo

Highlights: Explore interactive exhibits about Nobel laureates, peace efforts, and the history of the Nobel Prize. The center is housed in a historic building that adds to its significance.

Website: nobelpeacecenter.org

5. The Norwegian Museum of Cultural History (Norsk Folkemuseum)

Overview: This open-air museum features historic buildings and exhibits showcasing Norwegian folk culture, traditions, and rural life.

Address: Bygdøynesveien 36, 0286 Oslo

Highlights: The museum includes over 150 historic buildings, including a Stave Church, traditional Norwegian houses, and exhibits on folk art, costumes, and crafts.

Website: norskfolkemuseum.no

6. The Royal Palace (Det Kongelige Slott)

Overview: The Royal Palace is the official residence of the Norwegian monarch. It's an important historical and architectural landmark in Oslo.

Address: Slottsplassen 1, 0010 Oslo

Highlights: Visitors can tour the palace's grand rooms and see the Changing of the Guard ceremony. The palace is surrounded by beautiful gardens.

Website: slottet.no

7. Holmenkollen Ski Museum and Tower

Overview: Located at the famous Holmenkollen ski jump, this museum focuses on the history of skiing and winter sports in Norway.

Address: Holmenkollbakken 140, 0840 Oslo

Highlights: Learn about the evolution of skiing through exhibits and historical artifacts, and enjoy panoramic views of Oslo from the top of the ski tower.

Website: holmenkollen.com

8. Ekebergparken Sculpture Park

Overview: While primarily a sculpture park, Ekebergparken also offers historical insights, including ancient burial mounds and historical viewpoints.

Address: Kongsveien 23, 0193 Oslo

Highlights: Walk among contemporary sculptures in a historical park setting with views of the city and fjord, and explore the ancient burial sites and historical landmarks.

Website: ekebergparken.com

9. The Ibsen Museum

Overview: The Ibsen Museum is dedicated to Henrik Ibsen, one of Norway's most famous playwrights. The museum is located in the apartment where Ibsen lived for the last years of his life.

Address: Henrik Ibsens gate 26, 0255 Oslo

Highlights: Explore Ibsen's personal belongings and manuscripts, and learn about his life and work through exhibitions and guided tours.

Website: ibsenmuseet.no

10. Gamlebyen (Old Town)

Overview: Gamlebyen is the historic district of Oslo, featuring ruins and remnants of medieval Oslo.

Address: Ruins are located near the intersection of Bislett and Grønland

Highlights: Walk through the archaeological remains of Oslo's medieval fortifications and buildings, including the ruins of the old city walls and historical structures.

Website: byantikvaren.oslo.kommune.no

Local Tips

Get a City Pass: Consider purchasing an Oslo Pass, which offers free or discounted entry to many historical sites and museums.

Plan Ahead: Some historical sites require advance booking or have specific visiting hours, so check their websites before visiting.

Combine Visits: Many historical sites are located close to each other, so plan your visits to maximize your time and explore different parts of the city.

Public Transport: Use Oslo's public transport system to easily access historical sites spread across the city.

Oslo Philharmonic Orchestra

The Oslo Philharmonic was founded in 1919, initially as the Oslo Symphony Orchestra. It changed its name to the Oslo Philharmonic Orchestra in 1920. Over the years, it has developed a reputation for excellence and has become a cornerstone of Norway's musical culture.

Reputation: Known for its rich sound and versatile repertoire, the orchestra is recognized both nationally and internationally for its performances of classical, romantic, and contemporary works.

Conductor: The orchestra has been led by several renowned conductors over the years and is currently under the direction of a celebrated music director. The conductor plays a crucial role in shaping the orchestra's sound and programming.

Location

Venue: The Oslo Philharmonic performs primarily at the Oslo Concert Hall (Oslo Konserthus), which is known for its excellent acoustics and modern design.

Address: Fridtjof Nansens Plass 1, 0160 Oslo

Proximity: Located in the heart of Oslo, the Concert Hall is easily accessible by public transport and is within walking distance of many other cultural attractions and amenities.

Highlights

Repertoire: The Oslo Philharmonic's repertoire spans a wide range of classical music, including symphonies, concertos, chamber music, and contemporary compositions. It frequently performs works by Norwegian composers as well as international masters.

Recordings: The orchestra has a robust discography, with recordings of both standard classical repertoire and new works. These recordings have received critical acclaim and contributed to the orchestra's international reputation.

Performances

Season: The orchestra's season typically runs from September to June, with performances scheduled throughout the year. They offer a variety of concerts, including regular subscription series, special events, and guest appearances.

Special Events: The Oslo Philharmonic also performs special concerts, including collaborations with prominent soloists, composers, and conductors. They are known for their high-quality interpretations and engaging performances.

Education and Outreach

Educational Programs: The Oslo Philharmonic is involved in various educational initiatives, including workshops, masterclasses, and school concerts aimed at fostering a love for classical music among young audiences.

Community Engagement: The orchestra also engages with the community through outreach programs and free or discounted concerts for students and underrepresented groups.

Basic Facilities and Amenities

Oslo Concert Hall: The venue features comfortable seating, excellent acoustics, and modern facilities. It also includes amenities such as a café and an information desk.

Accessibility: The Concert Hall is accessible to people with disabilities, with features such as ramps, elevators, and designated seating areas.

Opening and Closing Hours

Box Office: The box office at Oslo Concert Hall is typically open on weekdays and before performances. It's advisable to check the official website for current hours and ticket availability.

Concert Times: Performances usually take place in the evening, with some matinee concerts scheduled on weekends. The exact timing can vary depending on the event.

Price

Ticket Prices: Ticket prices for Oslo Philharmonic concerts vary depending on the performance and seating choice. Prices range from affordable options to premium seats for special events. Discounts are often available for students, seniors, and groups.

Subscription Packages: The orchestra offers subscription packages for regular attendees, which can provide savings and guaranteed seats for the season's concerts.

Pros

High-Quality Performances: The Oslo Philharmonic is known for its exceptional musicianship and interpretative skill.

Diverse Repertoire: The orchestra offers a wide range of music, from classical staples to contemporary works.

Beautiful Venue: The Oslo Concert Hall is renowned for its acoustics and modern design.

Cons

Ticket Availability: Popular concerts can sell out quickly, so it's advisable to book tickets in advance.

Price: While there are affordable options, some premium tickets can be pricey.

Local Tips

Book in Advance: To ensure you get tickets to popular performances, it's a good idea to book well in advance.

Explore the Venue: Arrive early to explore the Oslo Concert Hall and enjoy its amenities, including the café and surrounding area.

Check the Schedule: The orchestra's schedule includes a variety of concerts, so check the program to find performances that align with your interests.

Combine Visits: Consider combining your visit to a concert with other cultural activities in Oslo, as many attractions are close to the Concert Hall.

Grace Bennett

The Ultimate Oslo Travel Guide (2025 Edition)

Chapter 9: Outdoor Activities and Parks

Hiking

Hiking in Oslo provides an excellent opportunity to experience Norway's famous natural beauty without venturing far from the city. The city's unique location, bordered by the Oslo Fjord and vast forested areas, makes it an ideal destination for outdoor enthusiasts. Trails vary in difficulty, from easy walks suitable for families to more challenging routes for experienced hikers.

Best Hiking Trails

1. Nordmarka

Overview: Nordmarka is a vast forested area north of Oslo, offering numerous trails of varying lengths and difficulties.

Highlights: Known for its beautiful lakes, dense forests, and diverse wildlife. Popular trails include the route to Ullevålseter and Sognsvann Lake.

Access: Easily accessible by metro (Line 5 to Sognsvann) or bus.

Difficulty: Varies from easy to moderate.

2. Oslomarka

Overview: Oslomarka is the collective name for the forests surrounding Oslo, including Nordmarka, Østmarka, Lillomarka, and Vestmarka.

Highlights: Offers a wide range of hiking options, from short walks to multi-day treks. Key destinations include the serene Lutvann Lake in Østmarka and the panoramic views from Kolsåstoppen in Vestmarka.

Access: Public transport connections to various entry points.

Difficulty: Varies from easy to challenging.

3. Vettakollen

Overview: A popular hiking spot offering one of the best views of Oslo and the fjord.

Highlights: The relatively short hike leads to a scenic viewpoint, making it a favorite for quick outings.

Access: Take the metro to Vettakollen station (Line 1).

Difficulty: Easy to moderate.

4. Grefsenkollen

Overview: A hilltop offering stunning views over the city and the fjord.

Highlights: The hike to the top is rewarding with a panoramic view, and there's a restaurant at the summit.

Access: Bus 56 to Akebakken.

Difficulty: Moderate.

5. Kolsåstoppen

Overview: A rugged trail that rewards hikers with breathtaking views over the Oslo Fjord.

Highlights: The trail passes through beautiful forests and rocky outcrops.

Access: Take the metro to Kolsås station (Line 3).

Difficulty: Moderate to challenging.

Essential Information

Best Time to Hike

Summer (June to August): Offers the best weather, with long daylight hours and comfortable temperatures.

Autumn (September to October): Beautiful fall foliage makes this a picturesque time to hike.

Spring (April to May): Pleasant temperatures and blooming nature.

Winter (November to March): Some trails may be accessible for winter hiking or snowshoeing, but check conditions beforehand.

What to Bring

Clothing: Layered clothing suitable for changing weather conditions, sturdy hiking boots, and rain gear.

Equipment: Backpack, water bottle, snacks, map or GPS, first aid kit, and a charged mobile phone.

Safety: Inform someone of your hiking plans, especially if going on longer or less-traveled trails.

Tips for Hikers

Trail Etiquette

Respect Nature: Stay on marked trails to protect the environment and avoid damaging flora.

Leave No Trace: Carry out all trash and leave the trails as you found them.

Respect Wildlife: Observe animals from a distance and do not feed them.

Navigation

Trail Markers: Trails are usually well-marked with signs and colored markers. Maps are available at tourist information centers.

Apps: Use hiking apps like UT.no or Oslo Hiking to navigate and find trails.

Local Tips

Public Transport: Oslo's public transport system is excellent and can get you close to many trailheads. Use the Ruter app for planning your journey.

Combine Activities: Many hiking trails are close to other attractions. Combine your hike with a visit to a local museum or a swim in a lake.

Pack a Picnic: Many trails have scenic spots perfect for a picnic, so bring some local Norwegian snacks.

Popular Hiking Events

Tour de Oslo: A popular event where participants hike through different parts of Oslomarka.

Kjentmannsmerket: A traditional Norwegian hiking challenge where hikers visit specific markers throughout Oslomarka.

Pros and Cons

Pros

Accessibility: Proximity to the city makes it easy to fit a hike into your itinerary.

Variety: A wide range of trails caters to all fitness levels and preferences.

Scenic Beauty: Stunning natural landscapes and views.

Cons

Weather: Oslo's weather can be unpredictable, so always be prepared for rain or sudden changes.

Popularity: Some trails can be crowded, especially on weekends and holidays.

Skiing and Snowboarding

Oslo is uniquely positioned to offer winter sports enthusiasts easy access to a variety of skiing and snowboarding options. The city's proximity to numerous ski resorts, coupled with its efficient public transportation system, ensures that winter sports are accessible to residents and tourists alike. From well-groomed slopes to pristine cross-country trails, Oslo caters to all preferences and skill levels.

Best Ski Resorts and Areas

1. Oslo Winter Park (Tryvann)

Overview: The largest and most popular ski resort in Oslo, offering a range of slopes for all levels.

Location: 20 minutes from the city center, accessible by metro (Line 1 to Voksenkollen).

Highlights: Features 18 slopes and 11 lifts, with a variety of runs for beginners, intermediates, and advanced skiers. The park also includes terrain parks for snowboarders and freestyle skiers.

Facilities: Ski and snowboard rentals, ski school, restaurants, and cafes.

Website: oslo.vinterpark.no

2. Grefsenkollen

Overview: A smaller ski area located close to the city center, ideal for a quick ski outing.

Location: About 15 minutes from the city center, accessible by bus.

Highlights: Offers a few slopes suitable for beginners and families. The area is also popular for its night skiing.

Facilities: Ski rentals, a cozy restaurant, and scenic views of Oslo.

Website: grefsenkollen.no

3. Korketrekkeren Toboggan Run

Overview: While not a traditional ski slope, Korketrekkeren is a popular toboggan run that offers an exhilarating experience.

Location: Near Frognerseteren metro station (Line 1).

Highlights: The toboggan run is 2 km long and provides a thrilling descent with a spectacular view.

Facilities: Toboggan rentals are available at the start of the run.

Website: korketrekkeren.no

4. Nordmarka

Overview: Nordmarka is a vast forested area north of Oslo, renowned for its extensive cross-country skiing trails.

Location: Easily accessible from multiple points around Oslo, including Sognsvann and Frognerseteren.

Highlights: Offers hundreds of kilometers of groomed trails for all skill levels, through beautiful forests and around picturesque lakes.

Facilities: Warming huts, cafes, and rental facilities at various entry points.

Essential Information

Best Time to Visit

Winter Season: The ski season in Oslo typically runs from late November to early April, depending on snowfall and weather conditions.

Peak Season: December to March offers the best conditions, with well-groomed slopes and reliable snow cover.

What to Bring

Clothing: Layered winter clothing, including a waterproof jacket, snow pants, thermal base layers, gloves, hat, and goggles.

Equipment: Ski or snowboard gear, which can be rented at most ski resorts if you don't have your own.

Safety Gear: Helmets are recommended for all skiers and snowboarders.

Tips for Skiers and Snowboarders

Choosing the Right Slope

Beginners: Look for green (easy) and blue (intermediate) slopes. Ski schools and beginner areas are perfect for learning the basics.

Intermediate: Blue and red (advanced intermediate) slopes offer more challenging terrain.

Advanced: Black (expert) slopes and terrain parks are ideal for those seeking more demanding runs and freestyle opportunities.

Safety and Etiquette

Respect the Rules: Follow all posted signs and resort rules to ensure a safe experience for everyone.

Stay in Control: Always ski or snowboard within your ability level and be aware of other people on the slopes.

Warm-Up: Take breaks to avoid fatigue and stay hydrated.

Local Tips

Public Transport: Oslo's public transportation system makes it easy to reach ski areas. Use the Ruter app to plan your journey.

Avoid Peak Times: Visit ski resorts during weekdays or early mornings to avoid crowds.

Combine Activities: Pair your skiing or snowboarding trip with other winter activities, such as a visit to the Holmenkollen Ski Museum or a warm drink at a local café.

Popular Skiing and Snowboarding Events

FIS World Cup Events: Oslo often hosts international skiing and snowboarding competitions, including the FIS World Cup events at Holmenkollen.

Local Races: Many local ski clubs organize races and events throughout the winter season.

Pros and Cons

Pros

Accessibility: Proximity to the city center makes skiing and snowboarding easily accessible.

Variety: A wide range of slopes and trails cater to all skill levels and preferences.

Scenic Beauty: Stunning natural landscapes enhance the overall experience.

Cons

Weather Dependence: Skiing conditions are dependent on snowfall and weather, which can be variable.

Crowds: Popular ski areas can get crowded, especially on weekends and holidays.

Ice Skating

Oslo boasts several ice skating rinks, both indoor and outdoor, providing excellent opportunities for skaters of all levels. Whether you're a beginner looking to try skating for the first time or an experienced skater seeking a scenic outdoor rink, Oslo has something for everyone. The city's ice rinks are well-maintained and offer a range of facilities to ensure a fun and safe experience.

Best Ice Skating Rinks

1. Spikersuppa Ice Rink

Overview: Spikersuppa is one of the most popular outdoor ice rinks in Oslo, located in the heart of the city.

Location: Situated between the National Theatre and the Parliament (Stortinget), along Karl Johans gate.

Highlights: The rink is beautifully illuminated in the evenings and surrounded by festive decorations during the winter season, creating a magical atmosphere.

Facilities: Skate rentals are available on-site, and there are nearby cafes and restaurants.

Opening Hours: Typically open from late November to early March, depending on weather conditions. Usually operates from morning until late evening.

Price: Free entry; skate rentals available for a fee.

Website: oslo.kommune.no

2. Frogner Stadium Ice Rink

Overview: Frogner Stadium offers a large outdoor rink suitable for both recreational skating and ice hockey.

Location: Located in Frogner Park, near Majorstuen.

Highlights: Known for its spacious ice surface and vibrant atmosphere. It's a great place for families and groups.

Facilities: Skate rentals, changing rooms, and a cafe.

Opening Hours: Open from December to February, with daily sessions from morning until late evening.

Price: Admission fee applies; skate rentals available for a fee.

Website: oslosk.no

3. Jordal Amfi

Overview: Jordal Amfi is an indoor ice rink that hosts ice hockey games and public skating sessions.

Location: Located in the Gamle Oslo district.

Highlights: Offers a sheltered environment for skating regardless of the weather. Ideal for those seeking consistent ice conditions.

Facilities: Skate rentals, locker rooms, and a snack bar.

Opening Hours: Open year-round, with specific times for public skating sessions.

Price: Admission fee applies; skate rentals available for a fee.

Website: oslo.kommune.no

4. Valle Hovin Ice Rink

Overview: Valle Hovin is a large outdoor ice rink, perfect for both casual skating and ice sports.

Location: Located in the Økern area.

Highlights: Known for its extensive ice surface, it's a popular spot for ice hockey and figure skating.

Facilities: Skate rentals, changing rooms, and a kiosk.

Opening Hours: Open from November to March, with daily sessions.

Price: Admission fee applies; skate rentals available for a fee.

Website: oslo.kommune.no

Essential Information

Best Time to Visit

Winter Season: The prime ice skating season in Oslo is from late November to early March, when outdoor rinks are open, and the weather is suitably cold.

Indoor Rinks: Available year-round, providing opportunities for skating regardless of the season.

What to Bring

Clothing: Warm, layered clothing, including gloves, a hat, and a scarf. Waterproof outer layers are advisable for outdoor rinks.

Skates: You can bring your own skates or rent them at the rink.

Safety Gear: Helmets are recommended, especially for children and beginners.

Tips for Ice Skaters

Choosing the Right Rink

Beginners: Spikersuppa Ice Rink and Frogner Stadium are ideal for beginners due to their friendly atmosphere and rental facilities.

Experienced Skaters: Valle Hovin and Jordal Amfi offer larger and more challenging ice surfaces suitable for experienced skaters and those interested in ice sports.

Safety and Etiquette

Respect Others: Be mindful of other skaters, especially in crowded rinks. Skate in the same direction as the majority to avoid collisions.

Stay Alert: Keep an eye on your surroundings and be aware of the rink's rules and guidelines.

Take Breaks: Rest periodically to avoid fatigue and reduce the risk of falls.

Local Tips

Check Conditions: For outdoor rinks, always check the weather and ice conditions before heading out.

Avoid Peak Times: Visit during weekdays or early mornings to avoid crowds.

Combine Activities: Many rinks are located near other attractions. Combine your skating trip with a visit to a nearby cafe, museum, or park.

Popular Skating Events

Christmas Markets: Many outdoor rinks, like Spikersuppa, are located near Christmas markets, adding to the festive atmosphere.

Ice Shows: Check local listings for ice shows and performances, often held at larger rinks like Jordal Amfi.

Pros and Cons

Pros

Accessibility: Easy to reach rinks via public transportation.

Variety: A mix of indoor and outdoor rinks caters to different preferences and weather conditions.

Festive Atmosphere: Many rinks are beautifully decorated during the winter season.

Cons

Weather Dependence: Outdoor rinks are subject to weather conditions, which can affect ice quality and availability.

Crowds: Popular rinks can become crowded, especially during holidays and weekends.

Conclusion

Kayaking and Canoeing

Oslo is uniquely positioned on the Oslo Fjord, surrounded by beautiful islands and scenic waterways that are perfect for kayaking and canoeing. Whether you're looking for a leisurely paddle through calm waters or a more adventurous route, Oslo offers a variety of options for all skill levels. The city's commitment to preserving its natural environment ensures clean, inviting waters and abundant wildlife.

Best Spots for Kayaking and Canoeing

1. Oslo Fjord

Overview: The Oslo Fjord is the most popular area for kayaking and canoeing, offering a mix of urban and natural scenery.

Highlights: Paddle past the iconic Oslo Opera House, Akershus Fortress, and Aker Brygge. Explore the numerous islands, such as Hovedøya, Gressholmen, and Lindøya, each with its own unique charm.

Access: Kayak and canoe rentals are available at various points along the fjord, including Aker Brygge and Bygdøy.

2. Bygdøy Peninsula

Overview: Bygdøy is a lush, green peninsula with calm waters ideal for kayaking and canoeing.

Highlights: Discover hidden beaches, and historical sites, and enjoy the serene atmosphere. The peninsula is home to several museums, including the Viking Ship Museum and the Norwegian Maritime Museum.

Access: Easily accessible by ferry from Aker Brygge or by bike.

3. Akerselva River

Overview: The Akerselva River runs through the heart of Oslo, providing a unique urban paddling experience.

Highlights: Paddle through the city, passing under bridges, through parks, and by historic industrial buildings. The river offers a tranquil escape within the bustling city.

Access: Kayak rentals and guided tours are available near the river.

4. Sognsvann Lake

Overview: Sognsvann is a popular recreational lake located north of Oslo.

Highlights: The lake's calm waters are perfect for beginners and families. Enjoy a peaceful paddle surrounded by lush forests and scenic views.

Access: Accessible by metro (Line 5 to Sognsvann), with kayak rentals available nearby.

5. Maridalsvannet

Overview: Maridalsvannet is Oslo's largest lake, situated just north of the city.

Highlights: Known for its clean, clear waters and beautiful natural surroundings. It's a great spot for a serene paddling experience.

The Ultimate Oslo Travel Guide (2025 Edition)

Access: Easily reached by bike or bus, with kayak rentals available in the area.

Essential Information

Best Time to Visit

Summer (June to August): The best time for kayaking and canoeing, with warm temperatures and long daylight hours.

Spring and Autumn: Also good seasons, though weather can be more variable.

What to Bring

Clothing: Quick-drying and layered clothing, a waterproof jacket, hat, sunglasses, and sunscreen.

Equipment: If not renting, bring a kayak or canoe, paddle, life jacket, and dry bag for personal items.

Safety Gear: Always wear a life jacket, and consider bringing a whistle and a first aid kit.

Tips for Kayakers and Canoeists

Safety First

Weather Check: Always check the weather forecast before heading out, especially on the fjord, as conditions can change rapidly.

Stay Informed: Be aware of local regulations and navigation rules, particularly in busy areas like the Oslo Fjord.

Skill Levels

Beginners: Start in calm, sheltered waters like Sognsvann Lake or Bygdøy Peninsula.

Experienced Paddlers: Explore the fjord and its islands for a more challenging experience.

Guided Tours and Rentals

Guided Tours: Consider joining a guided tour if you're new to the area or want to learn more about the local history and environment.

Rentals: Numerous rental services are available throughout Oslo, providing kayaks, canoes, and all necessary equipment.

Local Tips

Pack a Picnic: Many islands and lakes have designated picnic areas, so bring some local snacks and enjoy a meal in nature.

Combine Activities: Pair your paddling adventure with hiking or biking for a full day of outdoor fun.

Wildlife Watching: Keep an eye out for local wildlife, including seabirds, seals, and even the occasional porpoise in the fjord.

Popular Kayaking and Canoeing Events

Oslo Kayak Race: An annual event that attracts paddlers of all levels to compete in various races around the fjord.

Summer Kayak Tours: Many tour operators offer special summer excursions, including sunset and full-moon paddles.

Pros and Cons

Pros

Scenic Beauty: Stunning landscapes and unique urban views.

Accessibility: Numerous entry points and rental facilities.

Variety: Options for all skill levels and preferences.

Cons

Weather Dependence: Activities are weather-dependent, with conditions on the fjord potentially changing rapidly.

Crowds: Popular spots can be crowded, especially during peak season.

Cycling Trails

Oslo is a bike-friendly city with a well-developed infrastructure that includes dedicated bike lanes, scenic trails, and bike-sharing programs. The city's commitment to promoting cycling as a sustainable mode of transport ensures that both residents and tourists can enjoy safe and enjoyable rides.

Best Cycling Trails

1. The Oslo Fjord Route (Nasjonal sykkelrute 1)

Overview: Part of the National Cycle Route 1, this trail offers stunning coastal views and runs along the Oslo Fjord.

Distance: Approximately 180 km, though shorter sections can be enjoyed for day trips.

Highlights: Scenic coastal landscapes, charming coastal towns, and picturesque beaches. Key sights include the Oslo Opera House, Aker Brygge, and Bygdøy Peninsula.

Terrain: Mostly flat with some gentle hills, suitable for all levels of cyclists.

2. Nordmarka Forest

Overview: A vast forested area north of Oslo, perfect for nature lovers and mountain bikers.

Distance: Various trails ranging from short loops to longer routes of 50 km or more.

Highlights: Dense forests, serene lakes, and beautiful vistas. Popular spots include Sognsvann Lake, Ullevålseter, and Maridalsvannet.

Terrain: Mixed terrain with both gravel and dirt paths. Some trails are more challenging, ideal for mountain biking.

3. The Akerselva River Path

Overview: A scenic urban trail that follows the Akerselva River from the Maridalsvannet Lake to the Oslo Fjord.

Distance: Approximately 8 km.

Highlights: Historic industrial buildings, parks, waterfalls, and green spaces. Key landmarks include the Vulkan area and Mathallen food hall.

Terrain: Mostly flat and paved, suitable for all levels of cyclists.

4. Bygdøy Peninsula

Overview: A beautiful peninsula offering a mix of cultural sights and natural beauty.

Distance: Various routes totaling around 10-15 km.

Highlights: Museums (Viking Ship Museum, Fram Museum), beaches, and lush forests.

Terrain: Mostly flat and paved roads, ideal for leisurely rides.

5. Østmarka Forest

Overview: A popular area east of Oslo for mountain biking and nature rides.

Distance: Numerous trails ranging from 5 km to over 30 km.

Highlights: Rugged terrain, dense forests, and pristine lakes. Key areas include Østensjøvannet and Nøklevann Lake.

Terrain: Mixed terrain with challenging paths, suitable for experienced mountain bikers.

Essential Information

Best Time to Cycle

Summer (June to August): Ideal for cycling, with warm temperatures and long daylight hours.

Spring and Autumn: Also good seasons, though weather can be more variable.

Winter: Some trails may be accessible, but be prepared for cold and potentially snowy conditions.

What to Bring

Clothing: Comfortable cycling attire, helmet, gloves, and weather-appropriate clothing.

Equipment: Bike (rentals available in Oslo), water bottle, snacks, and a map or GPS device.

Safety Gear: Always wear a helmet and consider bringing a first aid kit and repair kit.

Tips for Cyclists

Choosing the Right Trail

Beginners: Opt for flat, paved routes like the Akerselva River Path or Bygdøy Peninsula.

Intermediate: Try the Oslo Fjord Route or longer sections of urban and forest trails.

Advanced: Explore challenging terrains in Nordmarka and Østmarka forests.

Safety and Etiquette

Follow the Rules: Adhere to local traffic regulations and trail signs.

Respect Others: Be courteous to pedestrians and other cyclists, and yield when necessary.

Stay Visible: Use lights and reflective gear, especially when riding in low-light conditions.

Local Tips

Bike Rentals: Numerous rental shops and bike-sharing programs (like Oslo Bysykkel) are available throughout the city.

Public Transport: Oslo's public transport system is bike-friendly, with most trains and ferries allowing bikes.

Combine Activities: Pair your cycling trip with visits to museums, parks, and local eateries.

Popular Cycling Events

Oslo Cycling Festival: An annual event featuring races, group rides, and cycling-related activities.

Tour of Norway: A professional cycling race that often includes stages around Oslo.

Pros and Cons

Pros

Scenic Routes: Beautiful landscapes and a variety of urban and natural trails.

Accessibility: Well-connected trails and easy access to rental services.

Variety: Trails suitable for all skill levels and preferences.

Cons

Weather Dependence: Cycling conditions can be affected by weather, particularly in winter.

Crowds: Popular trails can be crowded, especially on weekends and during peak tourist season.

Parks and Gardens

Oslo's parks and gardens are diverse, ranging from historical gardens with meticulously curated landscapes to expansive parks offering numerous recreational opportunities. These green spaces are spread throughout the city, making it easy for visitors to find a peaceful spot to unwind, regardless of where they are staying.

Best Parks and Gardens in Oslo

1. Frogner Park (Frognerparken)

Overview: Frogner Park is Oslo's most famous park, known for housing the Vigeland Sculpture Park.

Location: Majorstuen, west of the city center.

Highlights:

Vigeland Sculpture Park: Features over 200 sculptures by Gustav Vigeland.

Frogner Manor: A historic manor house located within the park.

Beautiful Gardens: Includes a rose garden with over 14,000 plants.

Activities: Walking, jogging, picnicking, and photography.

Facilities: Cafes, playgrounds, and public restrooms.

Accessibility: Easily accessible by tram and bus.

2. The Royal Palace Park (Slottsparken)

Overview: The Royal Palace Park surrounds the Royal Palace and offers a blend of formal gardens and natural landscapes.

Location: Adjacent to the Royal Palace, in the city center.

Highlights:

Royal Palace: Visitors can admire the palace and its changing of the guard ceremony.

Statues and Monuments: Various statues of Norwegian historical figures.

Pond and Wooded Areas: Picturesque pond and wooded paths.

Activities: Strolling, birdwatching, and relaxing.

Facilities: Benches, pathways, and a visitor center.

Accessibility: Centrally located, within walking distance from major attractions.

3. Botanical Garden (Botanisk hage)

Overview: A scientific garden managed by the University of Oslo, showcasing a wide variety of plants.

Location: Tøyen, east of the city center.

Highlights:

Arboretum: Collection of trees from around the world.

Rock Garden: Features alpine plants.

Palm House and Victoria House: Historic greenhouses with exotic plants.

Activities: Educational tours, photography, and plant study.

Facilities: Cafe, gift shop, and public restrooms.

Accessibility: Easily accessible by metro and bus.

4. Vigeland Park (Vigelandsparken)

Overview: Part of Frogner Park, specifically dedicated to the sculptures of Gustav Vigeland.

Location: Within Frogner Park.

Highlights:

Monolith Plateau: Central feature with a towering monolith sculpture.

Fountain and Bridge: Iconic sculptures and beautiful water features.

Activities: Art appreciation, walking, and picnicking.

Facilities: Same as Frogner Park.

5. Ekeberg Park (Ekebergparken)

Overview: A sculpture and national heritage park offering stunning views of Oslo.

Location: Ekeberg, southeast of the city center.

Highlights:

Contemporary Sculptures: Works by international artists.

Panoramic Views: Overlooking the Oslo Fjord and cityscape.

Historic Sites: Prehistoric rock carvings.

Activities: Hiking, sculpture viewing, and enjoying the views.

Facilities: Restaurant, cafe, and public restrooms.

Accessibility: Accessible by tram and bus.

6. Tøyen Park (Tøyenparken)

Overview: A large park near the Botanical Garden, known for hosting events and festivals.

Location: Tøyen, east of the city center.

Highlights:

Concerts and Festivals: Venue for major events like the Øya Festival.

Tøyenbadet: Popular swimming facility.

Green Spaces: Open lawns and wooded areas.

Activities: Walking, picnicking, and attending events.

Facilities: Playgrounds, cafes, and public restrooms.

Accessibility: Easily accessible by metro and bus.

7. St. Hanshaugen Park

Overview: A historic park offering a mix of landscaped gardens and natural areas.

Location: St. Hanshaugen, north of the city center.

Highlights:

Hilltop Views: Offers panoramic views of Oslo.

Pond and Pavilion: Charming pond with a picturesque pavilion.

Walking Paths: Winding paths through wooded areas and gardens.

Activities: Jogging, picnicking, and enjoying the views.

Facilities: Cafe, playground, and public restrooms.

Accessibility: Accessible by tram and bus.

Essential Information

Best Time to Visit

Spring (April to June): Parks are in full bloom, with pleasant temperatures.

Summer (June to August): Ideal for outdoor activities and events, with long daylight hours.

Autumn (September to October): Beautiful fall foliage and cooler weather.

Winter (November to March): Some parks remain accessible for winter walks, though many activities are limited.

What to Bring

Clothing: Comfortable walking shoes, weather-appropriate clothing, and sun protection (hat, sunglasses, sunscreen).

Supplies: Picnic blanket, snacks, and water.

Extras: Camera for capturing the scenic beauty.

Tips for Park Visitors

Planning Your Visit

Check Events: Look up any events or festivals happening in the parks to enhance your visit.

Peak Times: Weekends and holidays can be busy; visit early or late in the day for a more peaceful experience.

Respect the Environment

Leave No Trace: Dispose of trash properly and respect the natural surroundings.

Stay on Paths: Stick to designated paths to protect plant life and avoid damaging the landscape.

Local Tips

Guided Tours: Many parks offer guided tours that provide deeper insights into the history and features of the area.

Combine Visits: Pair a park visit with nearby attractions or museums for a full day of exploration.

Popular Park Events

Øya Festival: Held in Tøyen Park, this music festival attracts international artists and large crowds.

Christmas Markets: Some parks, like the Royal Palace Park, host festive Christmas markets in the winter.

Public Art Exhibitions: Ekeberg Park often features temporary exhibitions by contemporary artists.

Pros and Cons

Pros

Scenic Beauty: Oslo's parks and gardens are beautifully maintained and offer stunning natural landscapes.

Accessibility: Most parks are easily accessible by public transport.

Variety: A wide range of parks, from historical gardens to modern sculpture parks, catering to diverse interests.

Cons

Weather Dependence: Outdoor activities in parks can be affected by weather, especially during the colder months.

Crowds: Popular parks can become crowded, particularly during events and peak tourist season.

The Ultimate Oslo Travel Guide (2025 Edition)

The Ultimate Oslo Travel Guide (2025 Edition)

Chapter 10: Shopping in Oslo
Shopping Streets and Districts

Karl Johans Gate

Overview

Karl Johans Gate is Oslo's main shopping street and a bustling hub of activity. Stretching from the Royal Palace to Oslo Central Station, it offers a mix of international brands, Norwegian retailers, and numerous cafes and restaurants.

Highlights

Major Retailers: Home to flagship stores of international brands like H&M, Zara, and Mango.

Norwegian Design: Boutiques showcasing Norwegian fashion and design, such as Dale of Norway and Moods of Norway.

Historical Landmarks: Proximity to cultural and historical sites like the Royal Palace, the National Theatre, and Stortinget (Parliament).

Activities

Shopping: Wide range of clothing, accessories, and souvenirs.

Dining: Numerous cafes and restaurants along the street.

Sightseeing: Combine shopping with visits to nearby attractions.

Accessibility

Public Transport: Easily accessible via tram, bus, and metro, with multiple stops along the street.

Aker Brygge and Tjuvholmen

Overview

Aker Brygge and Tjuvholmen are modern waterfront districts known for their upscale shopping, dining, and cultural offerings. This area combines luxury boutiques with stunning views of the Oslo Fjord.

Highlights

Luxury Brands: Stores like Louis Vuitton, Michael Kors, and Hugo Boss.

Norwegian Design: High-end Norwegian brands and design stores, such as Moods of Norway and Ting.

Art and Culture: Tjuvholmen is home to the Astrup Fearnley Museum of Modern Art.

Activities

Shopping: High-end fashion, design, and jewelry.

Dining: Gourmet restaurants and stylish cafes with fjord views.

The Ultimate Oslo Travel Guide (2025 Edition)

Leisure: Waterfront promenades and contemporary art exhibitions.

Accessibility

Public Transport: Accessible by tram, bus, and ferry.

Bogstadveien and Hegdehaugsveien

Overview

Bogstadveien and Hegdehaugsveien are connected streets forming one of Oslo's most popular shopping districts. Located in the Majorstuen neighborhood, these streets are known for their diverse range of shops.

Highlights

High Street Fashion: International and Scandinavian brands like COS, H&M, and Lindex.

Independent Boutiques: Unique stores offering fashion, accessories, and home decor.

Seasonal Sales: Known for major sales events, particularly the Bogstadveien market days.

Activities

Shopping: Fashion, footwear, beauty products, and home decor.

Dining: A variety of cafes, bakeries, and restaurants.

Accessibility

Public Transport: Easily accessible via tram and metro, with Majorstuen station nearby.

Grünerløkka

Overview

Grünerløkka is a trendy district known for its bohemian atmosphere, vintage shops, and creative boutiques. This area attracts a younger crowd and is ideal for those looking for unique finds.

Highlights

Vintage and Second-hand Stores: Shops like Robot and Velouria Vintage.

Design and Craft Stores: Boutiques offering handmade jewelry, ceramics, and art.

Local Brands: Norwegian designers and independent labels.

Activities

Shopping: Vintage clothing, unique accessories, and handmade crafts.

Dining: Trendy cafes, bars, and restaurants with a lively nightlife.

Markets: Visit the Birkelunden flea market on Sundays.

Accessibility

Public Transport: Accessible by tram and bus.

Oslo City and Byporten Shopping

Overview

Oslo City and Byporten are two major shopping centers located near Oslo Central Station, offering a wide range of shops under one roof.

Highlights

Oslo City: One of the largest shopping malls in Oslo with over 90 stores, including fashion, electronics, and beauty.

Byporten: A modern shopping center with a focus on fashion, lifestyle, and dining.

Activities

Shopping: Clothing, electronics, books, and more.

Dining: Food courts and a variety of restaurants and cafes.

Accessibility

Public Transport: Directly connected to Oslo Central Station, making it highly accessible.

Steen & Strøm Department Store

Overview

Steen & Strøm is a historic department store located in the heart of Oslo, offering a premium shopping experience with a wide range of international and Norwegian brands.

Highlights

Luxury Brands: High-end fashion, beauty products, and accessories.

Gourmet Food Hall: High-quality Norwegian and international food products.

Historic Building: A beautiful and historic shopping environment.

Activities

Shopping: Luxury fashion, beauty, and gourmet food.

Dining: Upscale cafes and restaurants within the store.

Accessibility

Public Transport: Centrally located, accessible by tram, bus, and metro.

Local Tips for Shopping in Oslo

Tax-Free Shopping

Non-EU Residents: Visitors from outside the EU can claim a VAT refund on purchases over a certain amount. Look for the "Tax-Free Shopping" logo in stores and ask for a tax-free form at the time of purchase.

Opening Hours

Typical Hours: Most shops are open from 10:00 AM to 6:00 PM on weekdays, with shorter hours on Saturdays and limited opening on Sundays.

Extended Hours: Some shopping centers and major stores may have extended hours, especially during the holiday season.

Seasonal Sales

Winter and Summer Sales: Major sales usually take place in January and July, offering significant discounts on a wide range of products.

Pros and Cons

Pros

Variety: Oslo offers a diverse range of shopping experiences, from luxury brands to unique local boutiques.

Accessibility: Most shopping areas are easily accessible by public transport.

Quality: High-quality products, particularly in design and fashion.

Cons

Cost: Oslo is known for being expensive, and shopping can be pricey, especially for luxury items.

Weather: Outdoor shopping can be less pleasant during the winter months due to cold and snowy conditions.

Markets and Bazaars

Mathallen Oslo

Overview

Mathallen Oslo is a food market located in the Vulkan area, near the Akerselva river. It's a paradise for food lovers, offering a wide range of gourmet products, fresh produce, and street food.

Highlights

Local and International Foods: Stalls offering Norwegian specialties, cheeses, cured meats, seafood, and international cuisine.

Gourmet Products: High-quality oils, vinegars, spices, chocolates, and other delicacies.

Dining: Numerous eateries where you can sample dishes from around the world.

Activities

Shopping: Purchase gourmet food products, fresh produce, and specialty items.

Dining: Enjoy meals at the food stalls and restaurants within the market.

Events: Cooking classes, food tastings, and culinary events.

Accessibility

Public Transport: Accessible by bus and tram, with stops nearby.

Opening Hours: Typically open from 10:00 AM to 7:00 PM on weekdays and Saturdays, with shorter hours on Sundays.

Grünerløkka Market (Birkelunden Flea Market)

Overview

Located in the Grünerløkka district, Birkelunden Flea Market is a popular spot for second-hand items, antiques, and vintage finds. It's held every Sunday in the park of the same name.

Highlights

Vintage Clothing: A wide selection of vintage apparel and accessories.

Antiques and Collectibles: Unique antiques, retro furniture, and collectibles.

Handmade Items: Crafts, jewelry, and handmade products from local artisans.

Activities

Shopping: Browse through stalls offering a variety of second-hand goods.

Exploring: Discover unique and rare items.

Socializing: Enjoy the lively atmosphere and interact with local vendors.

Accessibility

Public Transport: Accessible by tram and bus, with stops near Birkelunden Park.

Opening Hours: Open every Sunday from 12:00 PM to 5:00 PM.

Vestkanttorvet Market

Overview

Vestkanttorvet Market is one of Oslo's oldest and most well-known flea markets, located in the Majorstuen area. It's a treasure trove for vintage enthusiasts and collectors.

Highlights

Antiques and Vintage Items: Furniture, home decor, and unique collectibles.

Books and Records: A variety of second-hand books, vinyl records, and memorabilia.

Art and Crafts: Original artworks, handmade crafts, and vintage jewelry.

Activities

Shopping: Hunt for vintage treasures and unique finds.

Exploring: Enjoy browsing through a diverse range of items.

Socializing: Engage with vendors and fellow shoppers.

Accessibility

Public Transport: Accessible by tram, metro, and bus.

Opening Hours: Open on Saturdays from 9:00 AM to 5:00 PM.

Blå Sunday Market

Overview

The Blå Sunday Market, located along the Akerselva river, is a trendy market known for its artsy vibe. It takes place at the Blå club, making it a unique spot for finding handmade and artistic items.

Highlights

Handmade Crafts: Jewelry, ceramics, textiles, and other crafts by local artists.

Vintage and Retro Items: Clothing, accessories, and home decor.

Food Stalls: A variety of street food options to enjoy while shopping.

Activities

Shopping: Browse through stalls offering handmade and vintage items.

Dining: Sample street food from various vendors.

Exploring: Enjoy the artistic and bohemian atmosphere.

Accessibility

Public Transport: Accessible by tram and bus.

Opening Hours: Open on Sundays from 12:00 PM to 5:00 PM.

Christmas Markets

Overview

During the holiday season, Oslo hosts several Christmas markets, offering a festive atmosphere with holiday decorations, gifts, and seasonal food and drink.

Highlights

Holiday Gifts: Handmade ornaments, crafts, and Christmas decorations.

Seasonal Treats: Traditional Norwegian Christmas foods, mulled wine (gløgg), and sweets.

Entertainment: Carol singing, performances, and activities for children.

Notable Christmas Markets

Spikersuppa Christmas Market: Located in the heart of the city, near the National Theatre.

Youngstorget Christmas Market: Another popular market offering a wide range of holiday items.

Activities

Shopping: Find unique holiday gifts and decorations.

Dining: Enjoy seasonal food and drinks.

Festivities: Participate in holiday activities and enjoy the festive ambiance.

Accessibility

Public Transport: Centrally located, accessible by tram, bus, and metro.

Opening Hours: Typically open from late November until Christmas Eve, with varying hours.

Grønland Market

Overview

Grønland Market is located in one of Oslo's most multicultural districts, offering a diverse range of products from around the world. It's a bustling area known for its exotic food stalls and international grocery stores.

Highlights

International Foods: Spices, fresh produce, and specialty foods from various countries.

Clothing and Accessories: Affordable fashion items and accessories.

Household Goods: Kitchenware, textiles, and other practical items.

Activities

Shopping: Purchase international foods and everyday items.

Exploring: Experience the multicultural vibe of the Grønland district.

Dining: Enjoy street food and snacks from different cuisines.

Accessibility

Public Transport: Accessible by metro, bus, and tram.

Opening Hours: Most stores and stalls are open daily, with varying hours.

Local Tips for Visiting Markets and Bazaars

Cash and Card Payments

Cash: Some smaller vendors may prefer cash, so it's advisable to carry some Norwegian kroner.

Cards: Most markets and stalls also accept card payments.

Bargaining

Flea Markets: Bargaining is common at flea markets, so feel free to negotiate prices.

Fixed Prices: At gourmet markets and larger stalls, prices are usually fixed.

Best Time to Visit

Weekends: Markets are typically busier on weekends, offering a lively atmosphere and a full range of stalls.

Early Arrival: Arriving early can help you find the best items before they're picked over.

Weather Preparedness

Outdoor Markets: Be prepared for changing weather conditions, especially in winter. Dress warmly and bring an umbrella if needed.

Pros and Cons

Pros

Unique Finds: Markets offer one-of-a-kind items, vintage treasures, and handmade crafts.

Local Culture: Experience local culture and interact with residents.

Variety: A wide range of products, from food to antiques.

Cons

Weather Dependent: Outdoor markets can be less enjoyable in bad weather.

Crowds: Popular markets can be crowded, especially during peak times.

Limited Hours: Some markets are only open on specific days or weekends.

Local Crafts

Local crafts in Oslo represent a rich tapestry of Norwegian tradition and contemporary design, offering unique souvenirs that reflect the country's cultural heritage and artistic innovation.

Types of Local Crafts

1. Rosemaling (Traditional Norwegian Painting)

Description: Rosemaling is a traditional Norwegian folk art involving intricate floral and scroll designs, often painted on wooden objects.

Typical Items: Boxes, plates, and furniture.

Where to Buy: Specialty craft stores like the Norwegian Crafts Shop and Norsk Folkemuseum's shop.

2. Hardanger Embroidery

Description: A form of whitework embroidery originating from the Hardanger region, characterized by its geometric patterns and openwork techniques.

Typical Items: Tablecloths, napkins, and decorative linens.

Where to Buy: Handcraft shops and specialty stores such as the Norwegian Crafts Shop.

3. Sami Crafts

Description: Traditional crafts from the Sami people, indigenous to northern Norway, including items made from reindeer leather, antlers, and woven textiles.

Typical Items: Sami knives, jewelry, and clothing.

Where to Buy: Stores specializing in Sami culture and crafts, such as the Sami Center for Contemporary Art in Karasjok or Sami craft shops in Oslo.

4. Norwegian Pottery and Ceramics

Description: Contemporary and traditional Norwegian pottery, known for its functional and artistic designs.

Typical Items: Bowls, mugs, vases, and decorative pieces.

Where to Buy: Local pottery studios and shops like KODE Art Museums, which often feature ceramics from local artists.

5. Wood Carvings

Description: Hand-carved wooden items, including traditional Norwegian motifs and modern designs.

Typical Items: Figurines, kitchen utensils, and decorative objects.

Where to Buy: Craft markets, galleries, and stores such as the Norwegian Crafts Shop.

6. Textiles and Knitted Goods

Description: Traditional and contemporary textiles, including hand-knitted sweaters, scarves, and blankets.

Typical Items: Norwegian sweaters (lusekofte), wool blankets, and scarves.

Where to Buy: Stores like Dale of Norway and local craft fairs.

Where to Buy Local Crafts in Oslo

1. Norwegian Crafts Shop

Overview: A specialized store focusing on traditional and contemporary Norwegian crafts, including textiles, pottery, and wood carvings.

Location: Central Oslo, often found in cultural districts or shopping areas.

2. Norsk Folkemuseum Shop

Overview: Located at the Norsk Folkemuseum, this shop offers a range of traditional Norwegian crafts and folk art.

Location: Bygdøy Peninsula, Oslo.

Highlights: Rosemaling, Hardanger embroidery, and Sami crafts.

3. Oslo City Museum Shop

Overview: Offers a selection of local crafts and art inspired by Oslo's cultural history.

Location: Located within the Oslo City Museum.

4. KODE Art Museums Shop

Overview: Features contemporary and traditional Norwegian ceramics and crafts, often from local artists.

Location: Although primarily in Bergen, they sometimes have collaborations or pop-ups in Oslo.

5. Grünerløkka Area

Overview: This trendy district has several independent boutiques and studios where local artisans sell their crafts.

Highlights: Unique, handmade items, including textiles, jewelry, and art.

Craft Markets and Fairs

1. Norwegian Crafts Fair

Description: An annual event showcasing traditional and contemporary Norwegian crafts.

Location: Various locations around Oslo, with details available on local event listings.

Highlights: Wide range of crafts from local artisans.

2. Oslo Christmas Market

Description: Held during the holiday season, featuring crafts, decorations, and handmade gifts.

Location: Various locations, including Spikersuppa and Youngstorget.

Highlights: Seasonal crafts and festive items.

Tips for Buying Local Crafts

Authenticity

Check Labels: Ensure items are genuinely handmade and come from reputable artisans.

Ask About Origin: Inquire about the craft's origin and the artist to ensure authenticity.

Quality

Inspect Details: Check craftsmanship, materials, and finishing for high-quality items.

Compare: Compare items to ensure you're getting the best quality for your budget.

Price

Budget: Be aware that handmade and artisanal crafts can be more expensive than mass-produced items.

Bargaining: While bargaining is not common in craft stores, markets may offer more flexible pricing.

Pros and Cons

Pros

Unique Items: Local crafts offer unique, one-of-a-kind souvenirs.

Cultural Insight: Crafts provide a deeper understanding of Norwegian traditions and artistry.

Quality: Many crafts are made with high-quality materials and craftsmanship.

Cons

Price: Handmade crafts can be pricey.

Availability: Some traditional crafts may be harder to find outside specialized shops and markets.

Department Stores and Malls

Oslo offers a range of department stores and malls that cater to various shopping needs, from high-end fashion and luxury items to everyday essentials and unique Norwegian goods.

Department Stores

1. Døgnvill Burger

Overview: While not a traditional department store, Døgnvill Burger is worth mentioning for its combination of retail and dining experiences. It's a great spot to relax after a shopping spree.

Location: Near Aker Brygge.

Highlights: Delicious burgers and a trendy, modern atmosphere.

2. H&M

Overview: A popular global fashion retailer offering affordable and stylish clothing, accessories, and home goods.

Location: Several locations in Oslo, including Karl Johans Gate and Oslo City Mall.

Highlights: Trendy fashion, seasonal collections, and home decor.

3. Magasin du Nord

Overview: A classic department store known for a wide range of products, including clothing, accessories, beauty products, and home goods.

Location: Karl Johans Gate.

Highlights: High-quality brands and a long history of retail excellence.

4. KappAhl

Overview: Offers a range of clothing for men, women, and children, known for its Scandinavian designs and affordable prices.

Location: Various locations, including in major shopping areas like Karl Johans Gate.

Highlights: Stylish and practical clothing options.

Shopping Malls

1. Oslo City Mall

Overview: One of Oslo's largest shopping centers, featuring a wide range of shops, restaurants, and entertainment options.

Location: Located near the central train station, in the heart of Oslo.

Highlights: Over 90 stores, including fashion retailers, electronics, and home goods. Also features a cinema and a food court.

2. Aker Brygge and Tjuvholmen

Overview: A vibrant waterfront area with upscale shopping, dining, and cultural experiences.

Location: Along the Oslofjord, accessible from the city center.

Highlights: High-end boutiques, art galleries, restaurants, and beautiful views of the fjord.

3. Byporten Shopping

Overview: A convenient shopping mall located directly above the central train station.

Location: Byporten, above Oslo S (Oslo Central Station).

Highlights: A variety of stores, including fashion, electronics, and specialty shops. Easy access for travelers arriving by train.

4. Storo Storsenter

Overview: A large shopping mall offering a mix of fashion, electronics, and dining options.

Location: In the Storo area of Oslo.

Highlights: Features popular retailers, a large supermarket, and various dining options.

5. Saturdays in Oslo (Sundays Market)

Overview: Although not a mall, this market is held on Sundays and offers a mix of local goods and artisanal crafts.

Location: Usually at Youngstorget or other central locations.

Highlights: Unique products, local crafts, and a lively atmosphere.

Local Tips for Shopping

Tax-Free Shopping

VAT Refund: Non-EU visitors can claim a VAT refund on purchases over a certain amount. Look for stores that offer tax-free shopping and keep your receipts.

Sales and Discounts

Seasonal Sales: Take advantage of sales during major shopping periods, such as summer and winter sales.

Discount Cards: Some malls and stores offer discount cards or loyalty programs.

Payment Methods

Credit Cards: Most department stores and malls accept major credit cards. Carrying a small amount of cash is also useful for smaller purchases or markets.

Pros and Cons

Pros

Variety: A wide range of stores and products to suit different tastes and budgets.

Convenience: Malls offer a one-stop shopping experience with various amenities and services.

Local and International Brands: Find both Norwegian and international brands in one place.

Cons

Crowds: Popular shopping areas can be crowded, especially during peak times.

Prices: Some high-end stores and malls may have higher prices compared to smaller boutiques or markets.

THE END!!!